MW01711569

THE SECOND TARGET BOOK OF FUN AND GAMES

THE SECOND TARGET BOOK OF FUN AND GAMES

compiled by

NICOLA DAVIES

A TARGET BOOK
published by
the Paperback Division of
W. H. Allen & Co. PLC

A Target Book

Published in 1985
by the Paperback Division of
W. H. Allen & Co. PLC
44 Hill Street, London W1X 8LB

First published in two volumes in 1974 by Universal-Tandem

Printed and bound in Great Britain by
Cox & Wyman Ltd, Reading

ISBN 0 426 10532 X

Contents

Acknowledgements

The Editor is grateful to the following authors, agents and publishers for permission to include copyright material in this compilation: Fawcett Books for extracts from 'Strange But True'; The Bodley Head Ltd for 'Snake Story', 'Tying up the Stones', 'The Remarkable Ox, Rooster and Dog', 'The Clever Boy', all taken from 'A World of Nonsense'; the compiler and Abelard-Schuman Ltd for poems from 'Tiny Tall Tales' compiled by Ennis Rees; the author and Faber & Faber Ltd for the poem 'The Rum Tum Tugger' and accompanying illustration from 'Old Possum's Book of Practical Cats' by T. S. Eliot; the author and Faber & Faber Ltd for 'How to make a Piggy Bank' from 'Presents and Decorations on a Shoestring' by Belinda Price; Macdonald Educational Publishers for extracts from 'Working with Paper'; Syndication International Ltd, for selected cartoons, quiz strips and picture puzzles; Mr Len Costa for 'Things' and the accompanying illustrations; Mr C. Ryan and Mr Abraham Rosan for miscellaneous humorous material; the author, The Bodley Head, Ltd, for the poem 'Toucannery' by Jack Prelutsky; the author and A. P. Watt & Son, Ltd, for the poem 'The Centipede' from 'The Wherefore and the Why' by A. P. Herbert; the author and the Reverend Melvin Lee Steadman, Jnr, for the poem 'Old Quin Queeribus' by Nancy Byrd Turner; the author, Faber & Faber, Ltd, John Johnson, for the poem 'The cheetah, my dearest, is known not to cheat' by George Barker; the author, Faber & Faber, Ltd, for the poem 'My Father' from 'Meet My Folks' by Ted Hughes; the author, Kaye & Ward, Ltd, for scientific experiments from 'More Science Magic' by Kenneth M. Swezey; Miss Marcia Hurst for miscellaneous illustrations.

Please note: the compiler and her publishers have made every effort to trace the owners of copyright material in this book; in the event that any queries arise regarding use of material in this work they will be pleased to make adjustments in future editions of the book.

Let's start with a laugh . . .

What's yellow, has 2 wings and 22 legs?
Banana United Football Club.

Army Instructor: 'Imagine you are advancing on the enemy and one of your ears is shot off. What would you do?'

Recruit: 'Because I am a soldier of the British Army and will gladly suffer pain, I would carry on.'

Army Instructor: 'Very good. Now you advance a few more yards and your other ear is shot off. What would you do?'

Recruit: 'Stop my helmet from falling over my eyes.'

Where does one find yokels?
Inside eggels

Knock, knock!
Who's there?
Lemmy
Lemmy who?
Lemmy in and you'll see.

Crazy Limericks

There was a young lady of Diss
Who thought skating was absolute bliss.
Till love turned to hate
When a slip of her skate
Made her finish up something like this!

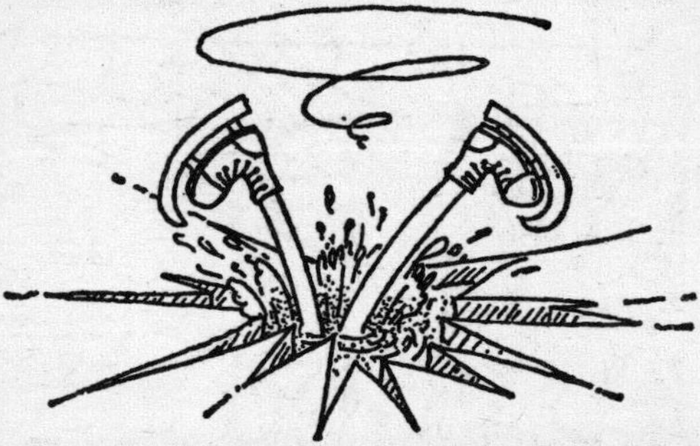

A major with wonderful force
Called out in Hyde Park for a horse:
The flowers looked around
But no horse could be found
So he just rhododendron, of course.

Plane Daft

There are eight differences between these two pictures. Can you spot them?

How to Make a Piggy Bank

You need: A round balloon; 2 sheets blotting-paper; 4 sheets tissue paper; 2 corks; 4 pipe cleaners; 2 ball buttons; a little felt; plastic fruit juice bottle; string; wall-paper paste

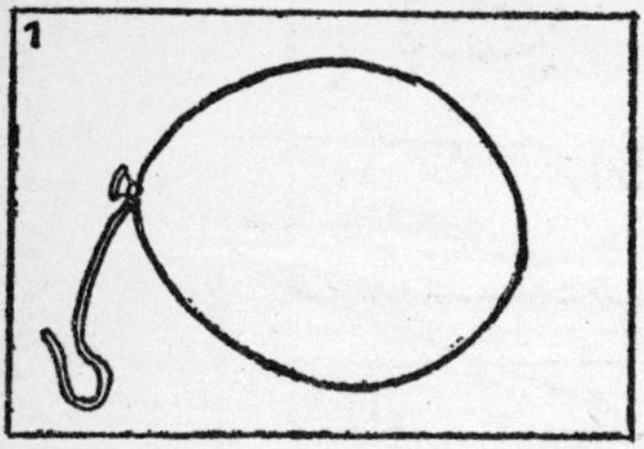

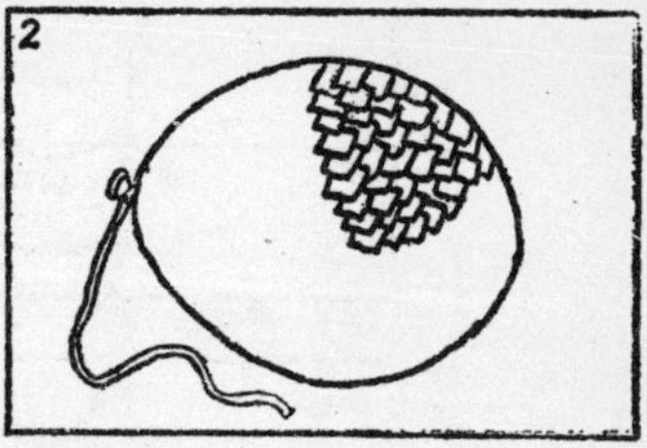

1. Blow up your balloon to the size you want your pig to be, and fasten it with string in a good tight knot, leaving about a foot (30 cm.) of string loose.

2. Cut or tear up your blotting-paper into roughly 1 in. (2·5 cm.) squares. Mix up some cellulose paste and stick the pieces of blotting-paper to cover the balloon, carefully making each piece overlap. Be generous with the glue as it helps to make a firmer body.

3. Now tear up your tissue paper and paste two or three layers over the blotting-paper, again making each piece overlap, and giving a final coat of paste over the last layer of paper. (If you use a different colour tissue paper for each layer, it will be easier for you to tell how much of the pig you have covered.)

How to Make a Piggy Bank

6

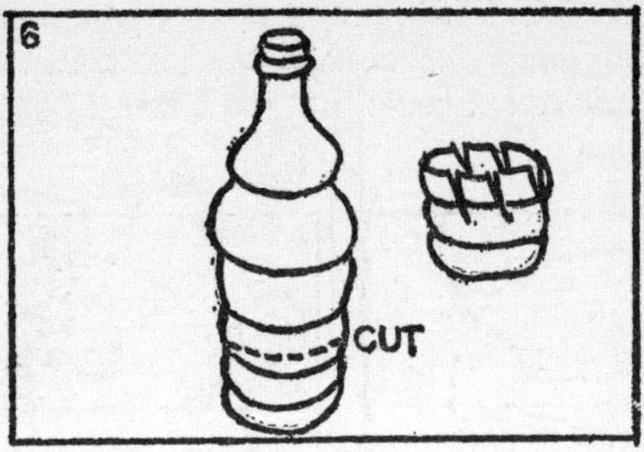

7

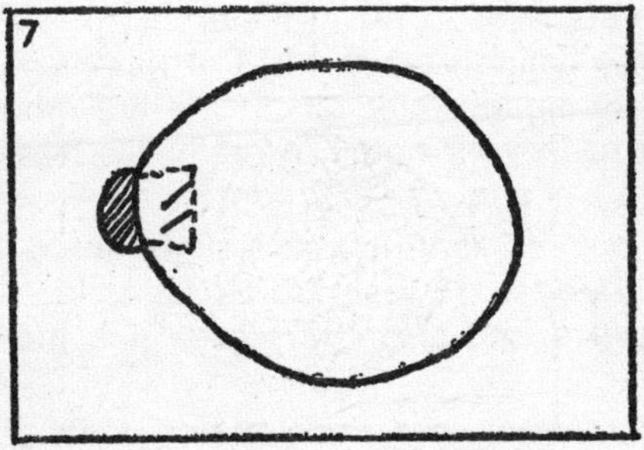

4. Next, hang up your balloon to dry in a cool place. If the room is too hot, the balloon may start to shrink. Leave well alone for 48 hours at least.

5. When you are quite sure that the paste is absolutely dry, undo the string around the neck of the balloon, and then pull your balloon out gently. It will come out cleanly and easily.

6. Cut about $2\frac{1}{2}$ in. (6·25 cm.) off the base of a transparent fruit juice bottle (from a chain store). This is to make a removable snout (which provides the easiest way of taking your money out of the pig). To make it easier to take the snout off and on, cut 1 in. (2·5 cm.) slits into the top or open end of the transparent base, keeping these slits about $1\frac{1}{2}$ in. (3·75 cm.) apart.

How to Make a Piggy Bank

7. Trace the cut edge of the bottle around the hole in the pig where the balloon came out. Cut this piece out very carefully. It is much better to cut the hole too small at first and try to fit your bottle in gradually, leaving about 1 in. (2·5 cm.) of snout sticking out.

8. Cut your two corks in half at a slight angle (25°) and position the body of your pig on to the corks. When you have balanced it into the right place, glue the corks on firmly.

9. Now decorate your pig. I put on two coats of a quick-drying lacquer paint, using a contrasting colour for the legs and the nostrils. (Remove the snout and paint it separately, so that it can dry thoroughly.)

With the snout off, I pierced two small holes $\frac{1}{4}$ in. (7 mm.) apart where I wanted one eye to be. I then cut a pipe cleaner in half and threaded one end of it up through one hole, through the ball button, down into the other hole and twisted the two ends together inside the pig to fix the eye securely. Repeat this for the second eye.

Next glue on two pieces of shaped felt for the ears. The tail can be made from three pipe cleaners twisted together and knotted on the inside so it cannot fall out. I cut out some flower shapes from doyleys to decorate my Piggy Bank. Now all that remains is to cut a hole in the top to fit your savings.

Apeing About

The words below are jumbled up. They all have APE in them, but can you arrange the other letters to make a word?

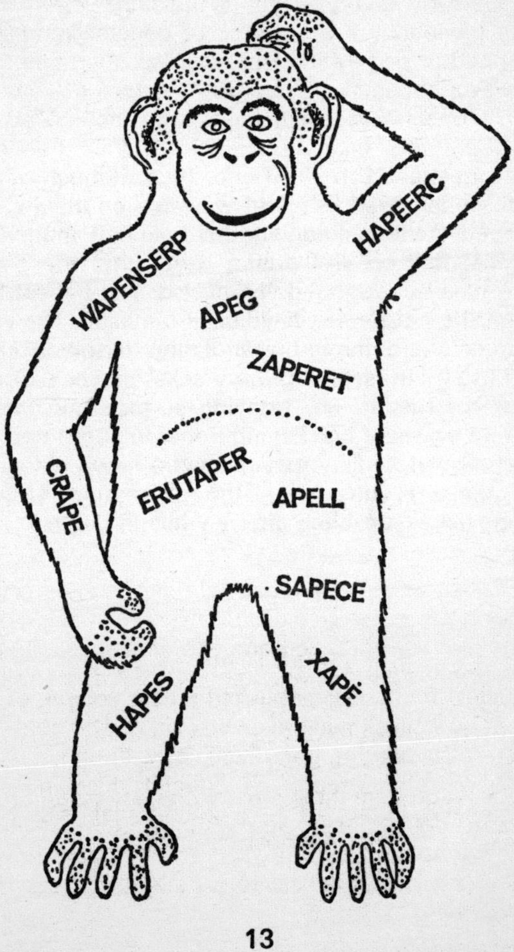

Astounding Facts

The Bald Truth

Being scalped wasn't always a fatal phenomenon during our forefathers' Indian fighting days on the American frontier. A victim could be cured of his plight, though the cure was nearly as unpleasant as the cause. Every frontier fort had somebody – a surgeon or general handyman – experienced at performing the remedial operation. It was done with a shoemaker's awl, ground to a narrow chisel point. The operator stood the awl on the victim's skull and twirled it between his palms to exert a drilling action. As the hole deepened in the bone, he cautiously reduced pressure. When a reddish fluid appeared on the awl point, he stopped. He then made another hole half an inch away and proceeded, on and off for days, until the patient's cranium was thoroughly polka-dotted. The patient felt no pain, but the noise must have been fantastic. The welling fluid spread and formed granulation tissue, a kind of 'proud flesh'; if the scalping was weeks' old, the tissue even penetrated beneath the decaying surface and lifted off paper-thin scales of blackening bone. In about two years, the flesh firmed and the patient had a new bald scalp. It was a bargain considering the alternative. Untreated scalpings usually resulted after a while in death.

Small Print

The smallest book ever published was a volume of Omar Khayyam quatrains, made in an edition of 150 copies by a Massachusetts printing firm. Each copy, bound in crimson morocco, was photographically reduced and weighed one-third of a carat. Fifteen of them could be laid side by side in three rows of five on a postage stamp.

Thing No. 1

JOIN THE DOTS

If you join all these little dots together what do you get?

Answer

One big dot.

Riddles Galore

Where was the first tree planted?
Right in the ground.

Who is a shifty person?
A furniture remover.

At what time was Adam born?
A little before Eve.

What is a stern necessity?
A rudder.

How can you make a jacket last?
Make the trousers and waistcoat first.

Why are Eskimos a mournful race?
Because they always have their daily blubber.

Why is a piece of toffee like a racehorse?
Because the more you lick it the faster it goes.

What tree is older than the oak?
The elder.

What are the highest buildings in the world?
Libraries. They contain thousands of stories.

Why can't you depend on a parachute?
Because it always lets you down.

Which Way?

The bricklayer is waiting patiently for the cement and the bricks, but the man on the left of the picture does not know how to work the complicated machine. When the sack hits the see-saw the tub containing the cement will go up so that the bricklayer can reach it, and at the same time the bricks will jump up and fall into the basket beside the bricklayer.

But does the handle have to go up or down to get the mechanism working?

Thing No. 2

BEES AND HONEY

Isn't Nature wonderful?

Do you realize it takes a bee 500,000 trips to your garden to make just 1 pound of honey? Backwards and forwards, backwards and forwards all day long, all through the summer. And as soon as he has filled one jar, screwed the lid down and stuck the label on – off he goes again to start on another one.

You'd think he would sometimes make a pot of jam, or a jar of marmalade, just for a change. But no. With bees, it's honey, honey, honey. All the time.

Isn't Nature barmy?

Balancing a Glass on a Pound Note

Can you balance a glass on a pound note? Sounds impossible doesn't it? It's quite easy when you know how. All you have to do is to fold the note so that it is corrugated. This gives it the strength to support the glass, which is balanced as shown.

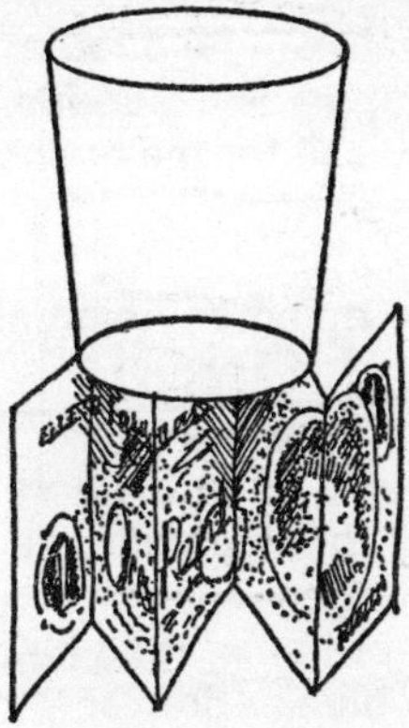

The Penny Out of the Wine Glass

Here is a trick that is easy to perform once you have got the knack. Put a penny in a wine glass and cover it over with a 10 pence piece. Then challenge your friends to get the penny out of the glass without touching the larger coin and without removing the larger coin from the glass.

Here's how: Hold the glass so that it leans towards you, then blow with all your might. The gust of wind rushes under the larger coin, lifts it up and throws it backwards. As it does so, its lower edge kicks against the far side of the penny and the force jerks the one penny piece out of the glass.

Try it before you show off so that you have some idea of how hard you need to blow.

The Rum Tum Tugger

T. S. Eliot

The Rum Tum Tugger is a Curious Cat:
If you offer him pheasant he would rather have grouse.
If you put him in a house he would much prefer a flat,
If you put him in a flat then he'd rather have a house.
If you set him on a mouse then he only wants a rat,
If you set him on a rat then he'd rather chase a mouse.
Yes the Rum Tum Tugger is a Curious Cat –
  And there isn't any call for me to shout it:
    For he will do
    As he do do
      And there's no doing anything about it!

The Rum Tum Tugger is a terrible bore:
When you let him in, then he wants to be out;
He's always on the wrong side of every door,
And as soon as he's at home, then he'd like to get about.
He likes to lie in the bureau drawer,
But he makes such a fuss if he can't get out.
Yes the Rum Tum Tugger is a Curious Cat –
  And it isn't any use for you to doubt it:
    For he will do
    As he do do
      And there's no doing anything about it!

The Rum Tum Tugger is a curious beast:
His disobliging ways are a matter of habit.

The Rum Tum Tugger

If you offer him fish then he always wants a feast;
When there isn't any fish then he won't eat rabbit.
If you offer him cream then he sniffs and sneers,
For he only likes what he finds for himself;
So you'll catch him in it right up to the ears,
If you put it away on the larder shelf.
The Rum Tum Tugger is artful and knowing,
The Rum Tum Tugger doesn't care for a cuddle;
But he'll leap on your lap in the middle of your sewing
For there's nothing he enjoys like a horrible muddle.
Yes the Rum Tum Tugger is a Curious Cat –
  And there isn't any need for me to spout it:
    For he will do
    As he do do
      And there's no doing anything about it!

How Many?

How many rectangles are there in this figure?

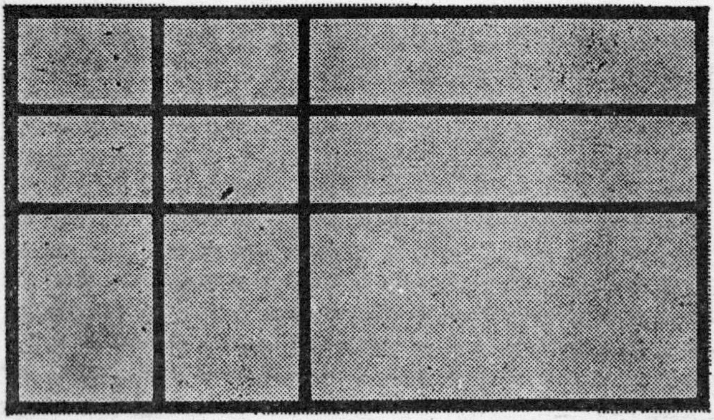

The Milky Way

The headmaster wants exactly 3 pints of milk in the dining hall immediately and I've only got a 12-pint measure, a 5-pint and a 4-pint one. I just can't work out a way to measure out exactly 3 pints.

Can you help me?

Thing No. 3

HOW TO DO PARACHUTING

1. Go up in an aeroplane.
2. Open the door.
3. Jump out.
4. Count up to ten.
5. Pull the . . .

Sorry. Go back. Start again.

1. Put your parachute on.
2. Go up in an aeroplane.
3. Open the door.
4. Jump out.
5. Count up to ten.
6. Pull the rip-cord.
7. Float down to earth.

(I hope I didn't upset you, forgetting one detail like that. It just goes to show how careful you have to be. Still, all's well that ends well.)

The Remarkable Ox, Rooster, and Dog

One day a man noted for his exaggerated stories told a friend that he had at home three extraordinary and precious things: an ox that could travel a thousand *li* (over three hundred miles) a day, a rooster that crowed at the beginning of every hour, day and night, and a dog that could read books. The friend said that he expected to lose no time in seeing such marvels with his own eyes. He promised to go the very next day.

The man did not expect this, as his home was somewhat distant, and he went home quite unhappily. He told his wife that he had at last got caught in his stories, and that he would be disgraced tomorrow when the friend arrived.

'Never mind,' said the wife. 'Leave things up to me and everything will be all right. Only you must keep out of sight.'

The next morning the visitor arrived and was met by the wife. He asked to see her husband.

'He is not here,' she replied. 'He has gone to Peking.'

'When will he be back?'

'In four or five days,' she said.

'Why, how can he return so quickly?' he asked.

'Oh, he went off this morning on our fast ox and can do it easily,' she said.

'I hear that you also have a wonderful rooster,' said the visitor – and by luck, just as he spoke, the rooster crowed.

'That is he,' said the wife. 'He crows at the beginning of each hour and he also crows whenever a visitor comes.'

'I would also like to see your learned dog,' he said.

'Ah,' she said, 'I am sorry. But you see we are very poor, so he keeps a school in the city.'

China

Joking Apart

Yesterday a man tried to tell the police that he was the invisible man, but they soon saw through him.

What goes peck, peck, bang!
A chicken in a minefield.

Teacher: 'This essay on "Our Dog" is exactly the same as your brother's.'
Johnny: 'Yes, sir. It's the same dog.'

How can you divide ten potatoes equally between seven boys?
Mash them.

Ist Man: 'I'll never marry again.'
2nd Man: 'Oh no?'
1st Man: 'No. My first wife died of poisoned mushrooms and my second from a fractured skull.'
2nd Man: 'Oh I'm terribly sorry. How did it happen?'
1st Man: 'She wouldn't eat her mushrooms.'

What lives in the sea and pulls teeth?
A dental sturgeon.

Customer: 'Beer please!'
Barman: 'Pale?'
Customer: 'No thanks, just a glassful to be going on with.'

Mixed Similes

Can you unmuddle these mixed-up similes?

As clean as an ox

As busy as a brush

As innocent as a board

As black as a bat

As sly as a new-born babe

As deaf as a daisy

As stiff as the ace of spades

As strong as the driven snow

As pure as a bee

As daft as a whistle

As blind as a fox

As bright as a post

Thing No. 4

AMAZING PUZZLE

Starting anywhere you like, can you see how to get to the middle of the maze?

Answer

Start from the middle.

More Astounding Facts

Funny Bunny

The news that a woman had given birth to fifteen rabbits rocked London in 1736, in a sensational controversy. Mary Toft, the wife of a poor weaver in a Surrey village, said that seven months before she had been frightened by a rabbit while working in a field. A London doctor, summoned by the village apothecary, helped deliver part of a sixteenth dead rabbit, he stated in a public report. With more rabbits expected, the king himself dispatched royal physicians to the scene while all London waited for further news and excitedly debated the case. What they saw led the king's sceptical physicians to bring Mary Toft to the city for observation. There the case soon blew up. A porter divulged that she bribed him to smuggle a rabbit to her, and under the doctor's browbeating, she finally confessed that the whole thing had been a hoax intended to win her a pension. For years afterwards, pamphlets describing the case were popular reading in Britain and choice accounts were collected into books – bound up, of course in rabbit skin.

The Mane Course

The lion as human food was never taken seriously by Europeans until, some years ago, a wily enterpriser capitalized on an old French saying. To comment on a bold act by some foolhardy person, Frenchmen would shrug and say 'He has been eating lion.' The businessman, himself a Frenchman, proceeded to can lion meat – or what he claimed as such – and sell it to timid people who wanted to grow brave as lions. He was reputed to have made $25,000 a year until the novelty wore off. As a matter of fact, many South African tribes occasionally eat lion meat, but usually cook the breast and throw the rest away.

Be a Sport

Fun With Cards

To place 4 Kings in different parts of the pack and bring them together by a single cut.

Take four kings and exhibit them fan-wise to your audience. But place neatly between the top two cards two court cards so they cannot be seen. When the audience have seen the kings, fold them together and place them quite openly on the top of the pack. Now take up the top card, which being really a king you may 'accidentally' let the audience see, and place it at the bottom of the pack.

Continuing your conversation, call your audience's attention to the fact that the next king which they must *not* be allowed to see, since it is not a king, is placed in the pack a little below the middle. Similarly with the next 'king', which is inserted in the pack a little higher up. Finally, take the fourth card which *is* a king and after exhibiting it carelessly, replace it on the top of the pack. In reality, you now have three kings on the top of the pack and one at the bottom.

Emphasizing the fact that the audience actually saw the four Kings separated as widely as possible, cut the pack, and after 'ruffling' the cards and shouting some magic word, let the audience examine the pack and find to their surprise the four kings all together in the middle.

'Ruffling' is simply the production of a short crackling sound by holding the pack firmly in one hand while the edges of the cards are slightly bent back, and then allowed to escape, by the fingers or thumb of the other hand.

Picture Puns

Can you guess from the pictures what the words are?
For example:

A butterfly!

Picture Puns

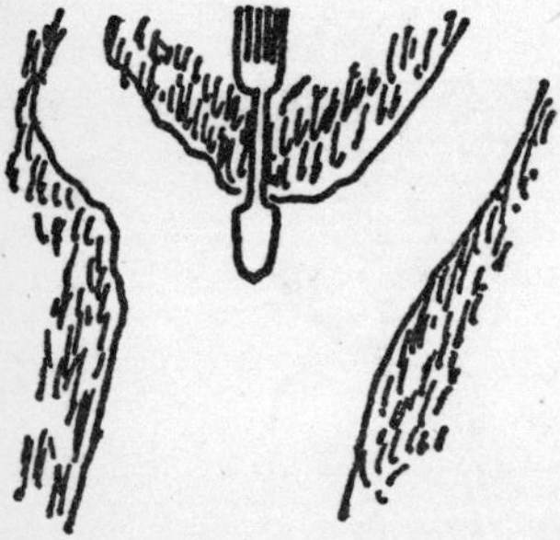

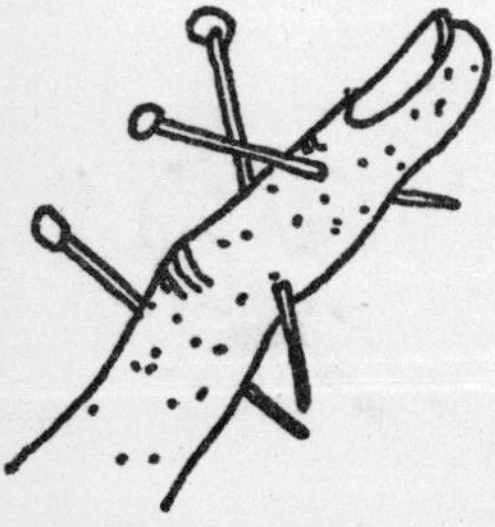

Read Any Good Books Lately?

On Top Of Nelson's Column by A. Pigeon

Haunted Houses by Denise R. Knocking

Vicious Lion by Claude Bodies

How to Keep Bees by A. P. Ary

The Lonely Princess by Mike U. Kry

My Famous Prison Escapes by Wilby Freeman

Woodwork Made Easy by A. Carpenter

Death in the Graveyard by May B. Slaughter

Mountaineering by Cliff Hanger

How to Get Rich by Penny Wise

Thing No. 5

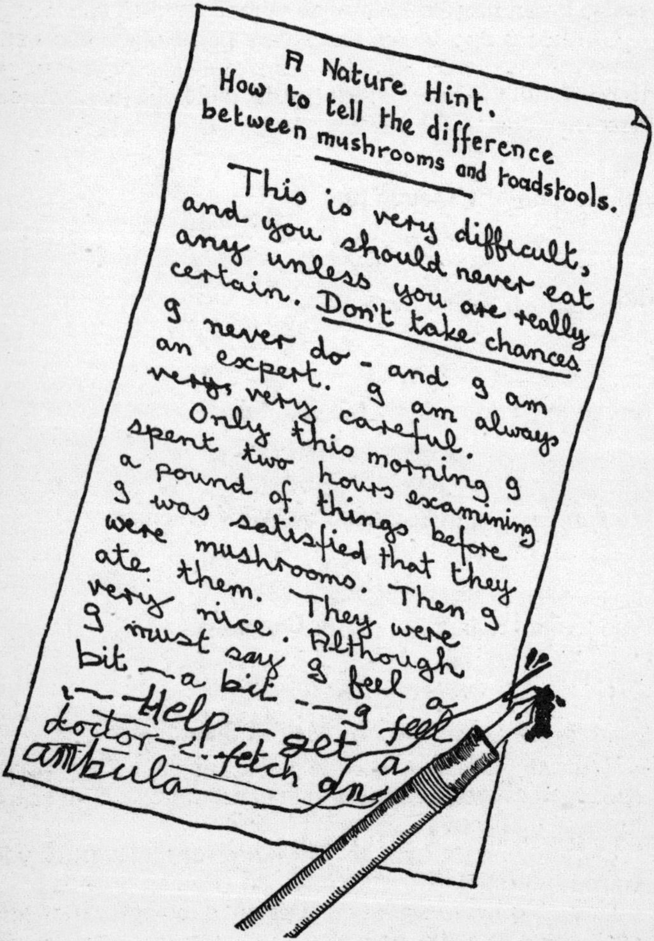
A Nature Hint.
How to tell the difference
between mushrooms and toadstools.
This is very difficult,
and you should never eat
any unless you are really
certain. Don't take chances
I never do - and I am
an escpert. I am always
very very careful.
Only this morning I
spent two hours escamining
a pound of things before
I was satisfied that they
were mushrooms. Then I
ate them. They were
very nice. Although
I must say I feel a
bit — a bit — I feel
— Help — get a
doctor — fetch an
ambula—

How to Make a Mask

Cut two eye holes in practically anything and you have a mask. It can be as simple or as complicated as you wish.

Cardboard egg boxes make very good ones, and here are some decorated. Attach a piece of elastic large enough to go round the head, making sure the holes are not too near the edge.

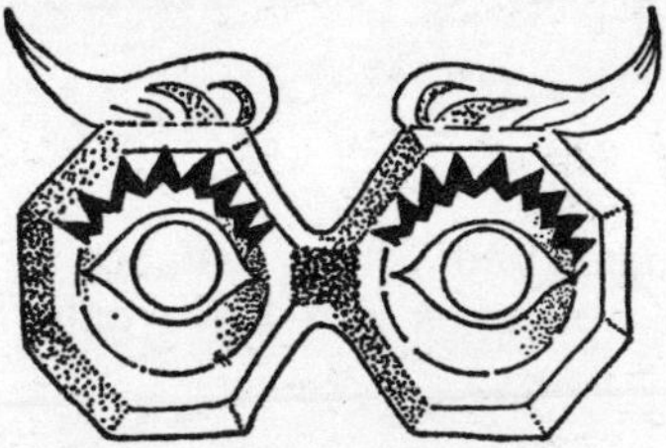

You can make masks with picnic plates, adding paper cups, egg cartons, pieces of thin cardboard, or bottle caps to make the features.

Start with a picnic plate. Cut holes for the eyes, so you can see, and a hole for the nose, so you can breathe.

Using big scissors cut two cups out of an egg carton and stick them into the holes on the plate for eyes. Or cut across the egg carton so two cups stay together, and cut so the centre ridge becomes a wonderful nose.

Matches to Puzzle With

Try these simple tricks on your friends.

Place eleven matches to make only nine.

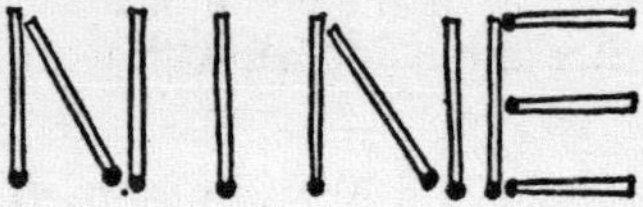

Form five squares with fifteen matches.
Remove three matches and leave only three original squares.

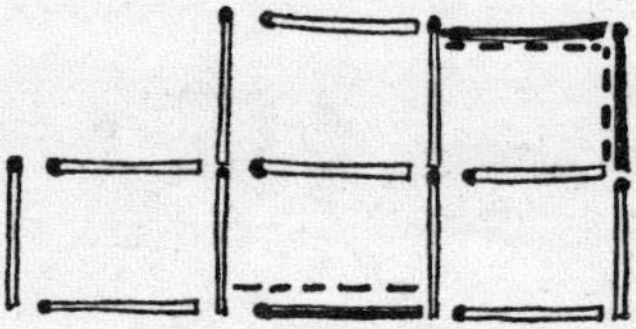

Place nine matches to make three dozen.

Howling Howlers

Every time Aladdin rang a Guinness sprang out of the ground.

James I died of an attack of the argue.

Not long after, the Invisible Armada loomed into sight.

Period furniture is furniture paid for from time to time.

Post Mortem means after twelve o'clock.

Some kinds of pimples are called blacklegs.

Boadicea fought herself and won.

Wolsey escaped death by dying on his way back to London.

John passed an interdict which forbad all births, marriages, and deaths.

Pompeii was smothered with saliva from the Vatican.

The Sewage Canal joins the Mediterranean and the Red Seas.

When vegetarians have decayed for several centuries they turn into coal.

Doodles

A giraffe passing outside a window

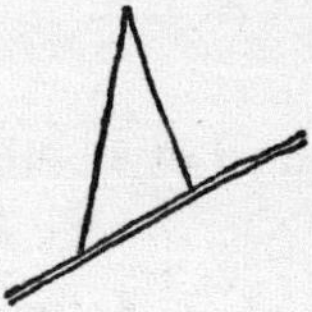

A witch coming up through a trap door

An ambush

A form to be filled

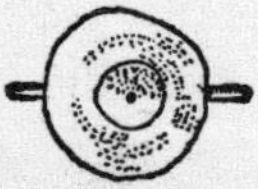

A Mexican on a bicycle

A spider doing a handstand

Up For Grabs

There are eight differences between these pictures. Can you spot them?

Doctor, Doctor

Doctor to Patient: 'Well, sir, I've got good news and bad news for you. The bad news is that we've amputated the wrong leg. The good news is that the other one's getting better.'

Patient: 'Doctor I think I'm invisible.'
Doctor: 'Who said that?'

Patient: 'Doctor, I keep getting the feeling I'm a horse.'
Doctor: 'Well, I can cure you, but it would cost you a lot of money.'
Patient: 'Oh money's no object. I won the Grand National yesterday.'

A doctor was called in to see a very testy aristocrat.

'Well, sir, what's the matter?' he asked cheerfully.

'That, sir,' growled the patient glaring, 'is for you to find out.'

'I see,' said the doctor, thoughtfully. 'Well, if you'll excuse me for an hour or so, I'll go along and fetch a friend of mine – a vet. He's the only chap I know who can make a diagnosis without asking questions.'

Doctor: 'Now, Mrs Smith, I think you are suffering from a split personality.'
Mrs Smith: 'No, we aren't!'

Doctor: 'I can't find much wrong with you. I'd put it down to too much drink.'
Patient: 'O.K. I'll come back when you're sober.'

Patient: 'I keep thinking I'm umpiring a cricket match.'
Doctor: 'Oh? How's that?'
Patient: 'Not out!'

Thing No. 6

HOW TO PLAY CONKERS – AND *WIN*

This is the Key

This is the key of the kingdom:
In that kingdom there is a city.
In that city there is a town.
In that town there is a street.
In that street there is a lane.
In that lane there is a yard.
In that yard there is a house.
In that house there is a room.
In that room there is a bed.
On that bed there is a basket.
In that basket there are some flowers.
Flowers in a basket.
Basket on the bed.
Bed in the room.
Room in the house.
House in the yard.
Yard in the lane.
Lane in the street.
Street in the town.
Town in the city.
City in the kingdom.
Of the kingdom this is the key.

Anon

In the Dark, Dark World

In the dark, dark world
There's a dark, dark country;
In the dark, dark country
There's a dark, dark wood;
In the dark, dark wood
There's a dark, dark house;
In the dark, dark house
There's a man trying to mend a fuse!

(A Children's skipping rhyme) *Anon.*

Thing No. 7

MUSIC QUIZ

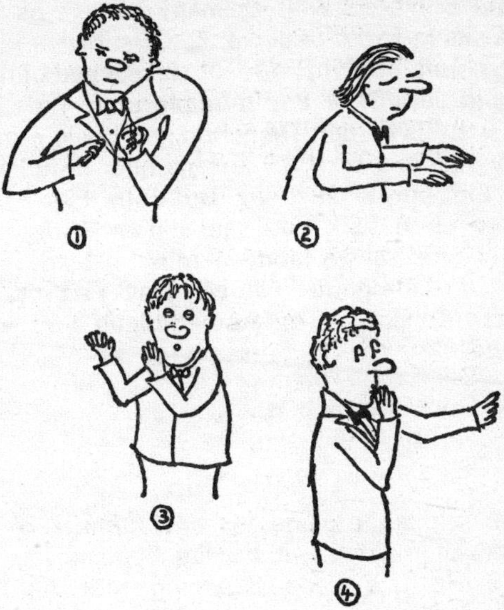

What instruments do these gentlemen play?

Answers

Man No. 1	None. He used to be quite good on the mouth-organ, but as you can see he has dislocated his left shoulder.
Man No. 2	None. I think he is sleep-walking.
Man No. 3	None. But he's very keen on fishing. He's not very good though – even the one he's describing above got away.
Man No. 4	None. And please don't make a noise. Ssssh! The baby over there has just gone to sleep.

Some Games

Fizz Buzz

This game is played with as many players as possible. Everyone sits in a row or circle. The first player in the row begins to count, but when the turn is reached of the player who would say '5' or any multiple of 5, he says 'Fizz' instead. 'Buzz' is harder. The taboo number is 7, and when 7, or any multiple of it, or any number containing 7 is reached, that player must say 'Buzz'. In 'Fizz-Buzz' both 5 and 7 are taboo, with 'Fizz' said at 5 and 'Buzz' said at 7. Any player who says a taboo number instead of 'Fizz' or 'Buzz' is out of the game. You can play 'Fizz' or 'Buzz' or 'Fizz-Buzz', depending on how difficult you want the game to be.

I Took a Trip

This is an alphabet game for any number of players. The players sit in a row, and the first begins by saying that he took a trip to a place beginning with 'A'. The next player repeats his sentence and adds that he *took* something beginning with 'B'. The third adds something that begins with 'C' and so on through the alphabet. However, each player must repeat everything that has been said by everyone else. Anyone who forgets a word is out.

Optical Illusion

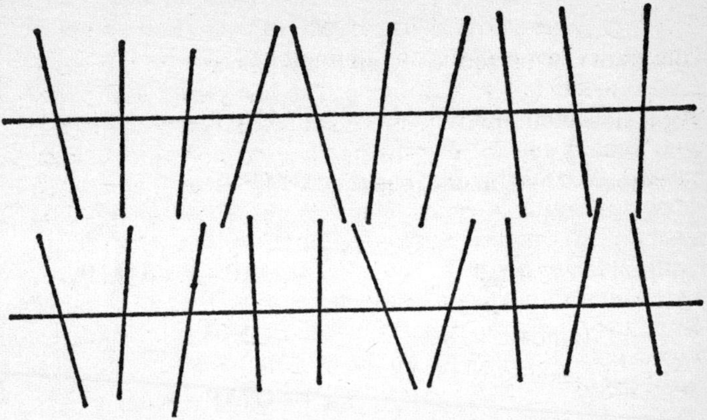

These railway lines don't look the same distance apart, but if you measure them you will find each rail is exactly the same distance apart everywhere.

As you probably know all visual impressions which the human eye perceives are upside down in the retina. This is due to the optical construction of the eyes, but we turn the picture round in the brain so that we register the picture as it actually is – the right way up. A scientist made a pair of spectacles which turned everything he saw upside down. At first he was completely confused, but it took him no more than a week before he began to see things correctly. He got so used to the spectacles that everything was again upside down when he took the glasses off.

UMP

The following words all have UMP in them. Can you work out what they are from the definitions?

A musical instrument	--UMP--
An impartial person who supervises a game	UMP---
He had a 'great fall'	-UMP-- -UMP--
Fat and rounded	--UMP
To wrinkle	--UMP--
Part of a cricket wicket	--UMP
This fairytale dwarf turned his name into a guessing game	-UMP-----------
An article of clothing	-UMP--
A camel has one	-UMP
To hit violently	--UMP

Thing No. 8

ETIQUETTE

How to Address a Red Indian

Or put it another way – 'To address a Red Indian' – 'How'.

That is to say, 'How'.

'How' is what you say.

How you say it is not so important.

But try not to make it sound like 'How?', with a question mark after it.

It might confuse him.

Decoding

Can you decipher these secret codes?

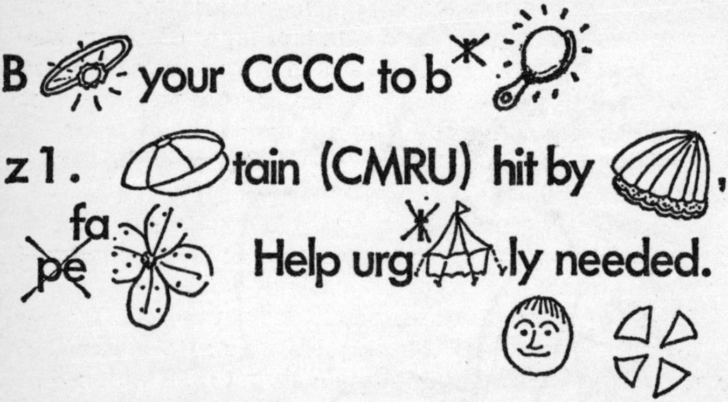

The Clever Boy

There was a man who could tell bigger stories than anyone else. One day he went out with his cow and said he would give her to anyone who could beat him at story telling. He went round among the neighbours, but none of them could win against him. Late that night he came to a hut where he found a little boy asleep. He asked the boy for a coal to light up his pipe. The boy started to shake the fire up and down, and the man got tired waiting.

'Little boy, what are you doing with that fire?' he asked impatiently.

'I am separating today's fire from yesterday's, and yesterday's from day before yesterday's, to give you the hottest coal,' said the boy.

'Little boy, give me some water,' the man said.

'All right,' answered the boy. He began to shake the water jar up and down, until the man got tired waiting.

'Why don't you give me the water?' he asked.

'I am separating today's water from yesterday's, and yesterday's from day before yesterday's, to give you the freshest water,' said the boy.

'Have you a mother?' asked the man.

'Yes, sir,' said the boy.

'Where is she?'

'She has gone with her needle and thread to sew up a hole in the king's palace that the wind tore in it last night.'

'What!' said the man. 'And where is your father?'

'He has taken a pot with a hole in it to the river to get water to throw on the land to make a garden.'

'Little boy,' said the man, 'did you hear that a child was born last night, with seven arms and seven necks?'

'No, sir,' said the boy, 'but this morning when I went to the spring for water I saw a shirt on the line with seven sleeves and seven collars. I think it must have belonged to that baby.'

The Clever Boy

'Little boy,' said the man, 'did you hear that last week a donkey took a trip into the sky?'

'No, sir,' said the boy, 'but last week when I went to the spring for water I heard a clap of thunder, and when I looked up I saw a packsaddle falling down from the sky. I think it must have belonged to that mule.'

'Little boy,' said the man, 'did you hear that the river caught fire last week?'

'No, sir,' said the boy, 'but when I went fishing last week I caught a lot of fish burnt on one side and raw on the other. I think they must have been cooked when the river caught fire.'

'Take my cow, little boy,' said the man. 'You are the cleverest fellow I ever saw.'

Portugal

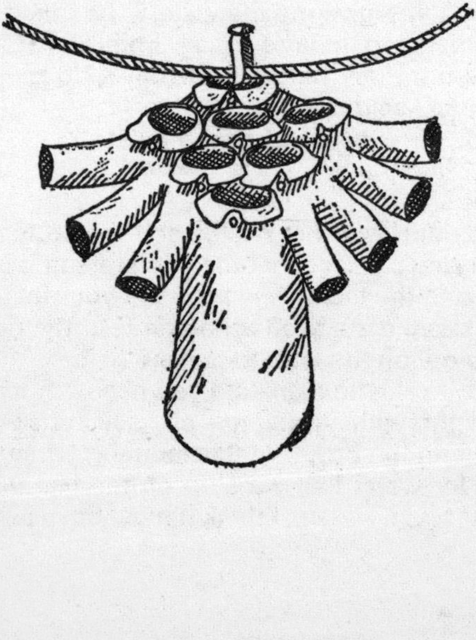

Riddle Mania

When is laughing dangerous?
When you split your sides.

Why is the letter V like an angry bull?
Because it comes after U.

What gets wet as it dries?
A towel.

How does a stove feel when full of coal?
Grateful.

What word is never pronounced right?
Wrong.

What is always invisible, yet never out of sight?
The letter S.

Why do boys always come before girls?
Because B always comes before G.

What is the world's biggest moth?
The mammoth.

Why is a boring speaker like a whale?
He often rises to spout.

What can you put in a dish but never get out?
A crack

Inspector Markham Investigates

Thing No. 9

A BALANCING TRICK

1. Tie a rope from the top of one tall tree to the top of another tall tree.
2. Climb the tree and walk along to the middle of the rope.
3. Hold your hand out flat and balance a candle on it.
4. Your friends will be amazed.

There's a trick in it of course. Here's how you do it:

Before you start, fix a two-inch nail into the bottom of the candle so that about an inch of the nail sticks out.

You can grip the nail between your second and third fingers and it will look – from the ground – as if you are balancing the candle on your hand!

The Floating Needle

You show a tumbler full of water and ask whether it is possible to float a needle on the surface. When everybody says it cannot be done, or tries and fails, you show them how easy it is. It is performed by first laying the needle on a small piece of tissue paper, and then floating them together on the water. The paper soon becomes sodden and sinks to the bottom, leaving the needle still floating.

The Penny Through the Hole

Take an ordinary piece of writing paper and in the middle of it cut a hole exactly the size of a penny. The trick is to slip a penny through the hole. Can't be done? Oh, yes, it can. After your friends have all tried and failed – of course they mustn't tear the paper or make the hole bigger – show them how it is done.

You must fold the paper across so that the crease goes across the centre of the hole. Then hold the paper by the four corners, two in each hand, so that it is sagging just a little in the middle, and ask someone to drop the penny on the paper. When the penny has come over the hole, draw your two hands nearer and nearer together and the coin will gradually go through the space.

An Arresting Story

Try, Try Again

The most frustrated prisoner in criminal annals probably was Dr Arthur Waite, a New York dentist who in 1916 tried to kill his wealthy parents-in-law by the novel method of dosing them with disease germs. To his mother-in-law, Waite fed a total of six tubes of pneumonia, influenza, and diphtheria germ cultures, mixed in her food; the elderly woman merely became slightly ill. Waite tried the same three diseases on his father-in-law, to no effect; then after giving the old man calomel pills to lower his resistance, he had his victim use a throat spray loaded with typhoid. The old man remained healthy. In desperation, Waite discarded germs and resorted to arsenic. Though it proved to be Waite's undoing – a suspicious relative ordered the father-in-law's body autopsied – this also failed him. At his trial Waite confessed that he finally had to smother his distressed victim with a pillow.

Chinese Delicacy

The last Manchu rulers of China clung to backward and sometimes barbaric beliefs. According to an old Chinese superstition, an ill person could get well by eating the flesh of a near relative or friend. When early in the 1890s the Empress dowager Tzu-Hsi became ill and feared she would die, her young nephew, the Emperor, came to her bedside attended by the chief eunoch and palace manager, Li Lien-Ying. The Empress complained that nobody cared enough to give her the only medicine that would cure her. A little later, she grew well. Li, away from his work and confined to bed, was found to have cut from his thigh a piece of flesh which had been cooked and given to the Empress in her food. The chief eunoch's singular act of devotion won him the Empress's favour and great influence in the Manchu government before it was finally overthrown by the Chinese Republic.

More Limericks

A bandy-legged policeman from Kew
Said, 'I really don't know what to do.
I can stop without fuss
A lorry or bus
But minis just simply go through.'

There was a young airman called Rutter
Who wanted to fly to Calcutter.
He began with a bang
A crash and a clang
But the furthest he got was the gutter.

Thing No. 10

A THING FOR NATURE-LOVERS

You are very lucky if you have hedgehogs in your garden because they eat snails and slugs. It's hard to believe, I know, but they eat snails and slugs because they like them. In fact, they prefer them to anything else. And as snails and slugs do a lot of damage to seeds and plants, the hedgehogs are really the gardener's friends.

So why not do something in return?
Here are two suggestions:

1. Hedgehogs usually come out only at night, and it can't be very pleasant for them. I bet they keep tripping over things or banging into trees. Why not fix up a few lights to help them see where they are going?
2. People who like birds often build bird-tables for them. Why not build a hedgehog table?

How to Make a Pirana Fish
(in paper)

Materials: Green paper, shiny coloured paper, glue.

Cut a square out of green paper.

Keep folding it as shown on these pages. Then open it up and fold the corners. It should now form a small table. Fold the table along one of the diagonal lines so one diagonal point touches the other, and stick the two halves together.

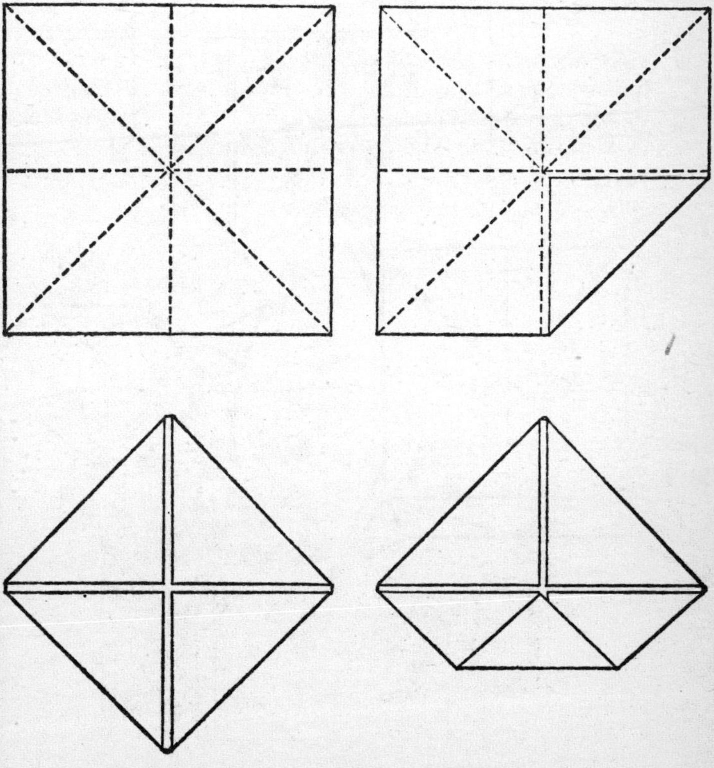

How to Make a Pirana Fish

Let the glue dry and then lightly pull outwards from the corners to make the pirana's mouth close. Decorate the fish with coloured shiny paper.

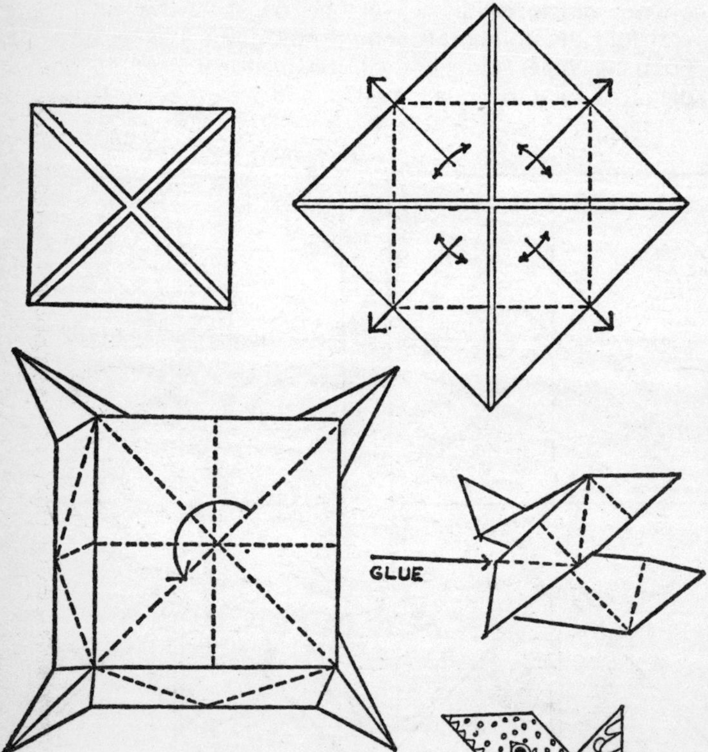

What Would You Like to Drink?

Would you like a glass of milk, apple juice, or water? Here we have the cow, the apple tree, and the pump, but which pipe leads to which glass? Look at the picture for 30 seconds and see if you can work out which of the glasses contains which liquid.

Idiotica

Did you hear about the idiot who bought a tie and took it back to the shop because it was too tight?

Lady on submarine: 'Captain, doesn't your gun get wet when you submerge?'

Captain: 'No, madam. We have a sailor to hold an umbrella over it.'

Did you hear about the two idiotic terrorists who were driving along with a bomb on the back seat of their car. Suddenly, they went over a bump. 'Careful,' said one of them, 'if we go over many more bumps like that the bomb will explode.' 'Don't worry,' said the other. 'There's another bomb in the boot!'

How do you confuse an idiotic road digger?
Lay out three spades and tell him to take his pick.

Does a silly robot have a screw loose?

Did you hear about the thick terrorist who when told to blow up an ocean-going liner said he couldn't because his mouth wouldn't fit over the funnels?

Did you hear about the idiotic driver who drove over a cliff to see if his air brakes worked?

Two idiots decided to go to the sun. When it was pointed out that they would get burned up, one of them said, 'Oh, no, we won't. We're going at night!'

How do you confuse an idiot?
Put him in a cylindrical building and tell him to stand in the corner.

A Military Parade

These soldiers are on parade and should all look the same, but in fact only two of them are identical. Can you see which two?

Thing No. 11

A PUZZLE

Madge, Simon, Len, and Sarah have got their kite strings all tangled up. Can you sort out which kite belongs to who?

On the other hand, why should you? It's their own silly fault – standing so close together like that, it's not surprising the strings got all jumbled up.

No. You leave them to sort it out, and it jolly well serves them right.

In Other Words

In these sentences you will find hidden trees. Do you know what they are?

Has he arrived?

The brush must be soaked in water.

There were UFOs from another planet in the sky.

The spinet is an instrument like a small harpsichord.

A mariner with a tanned face stood at the helm.

Will owed a great deal of money to his father.

Now try and find some fish.

Susan inherited her rings from her grandmother.

As Kate left she waved good-bye.

The ship had docked the previous night.

We drove directly to the car park.

All around the town the heads were displayed on spikes.

Triangles

How many triangles are there in this figure?

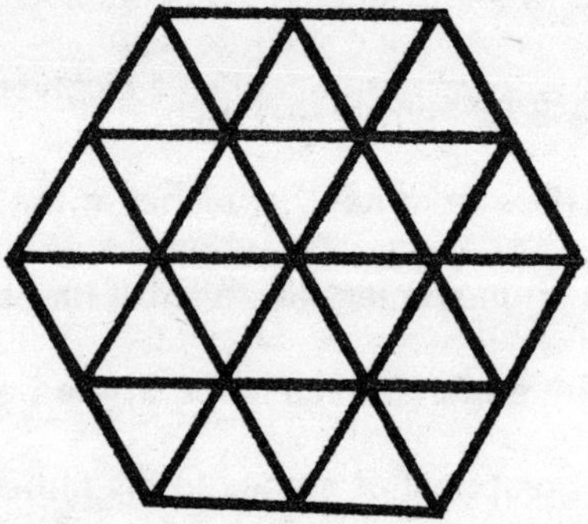

An Odd Problem

'Hey, you can't turn out in odd socks like that – one green and one white. You must have a pair.'

'It's not my fault. The light bulb is broken in the changing room and the socks are all jumbled up in the locker, and I couldn't see what I was getting.'

How many socks must he fetch out to make sure he has a pair?

Little Billee
W. M. Thackeray

There were three sailors of Bristol city
Who took a boat and went to sea.
But first with beef and captain's biscuits
And pickled pork they loaded she.

There was gorging Jack and guzzling Jimmy,
And the youngest he was little Billee.
Now when they got as far as the Equator
They'd nothing left but one split pea.

Says gorging Jack to guzzling Jimmy,
'I am extremely hungaree.'
To gorging Jack says guzzling Jimmy,
'We've nothing left, us must eat we.'

Says gorging Jack to guzzling Jimmy,
'With one another we shouldn't agree!
There's little Bill, he's young and tender,
We're old and tough, so let's eat he.'

'Oh! Billy, we're going to kill and eat you,
So undo the button of your chemie.'
When Bill received this information
He used his pocket handkerchie.

'First let me say my catechism,
Which my poor mammy taught to me.'
'Make haste, make haste,' says guzzling Jimmy,
While Jack pulled out his snickersnee.

So Billy went up to the main-top gallant mast,
And down he fell on his bended knee.
He scarce had come to the twelfth commandment
When up he jumps, 'There's land I see:

'Jerusalem and Madagascar,
And North and South Amerikee:
There's the British flag a-riding at anchor,
With Admiral Napier, K.C.B.'

So when they got aboard of the Admiral's,
He hanged fat Jack and flogged Jimmee;
But as for little Bill he made him
The Captain of a Seventy-three.

Pins 'n Beads

Simple props are used in this trick. You show three large safety pins on each of which has been threaded a different coloured bead.

Someone hands you one of these pins behind your back, hiding up the other two – you are immediately able to tell him what colour the bead is.

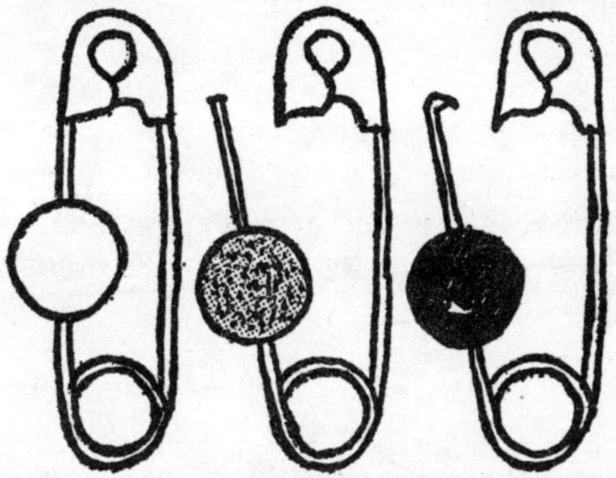

Look at the diagram and you will see how it is done. One pin has the point blunted (easily done with a file) the second pin has the point slightly curled over (do this with pliers) whilst the third pin is left normal. They are shown exaggerated in the drawing to illustrate the points.

When the pin is presented to you behind your back you secretly open it – feel its point which will immediately tell you the colour of the bead. You have of course memorized which is which.

Coloured ribbons tied round the pins will serve instead of beads.

Thing No. 12

2 RIDDLES

1. Q. What goes up a chimney down, but won't go down a chimney up?

   A. An umbrella.

2. Q. What makes your dad go red in the face, get violent, roar with rage and stop your pocket money for three weeks?

   A. When you experiment with his umbrella, trying to push it down a chimney up, breaking the spokes and ripping the silk cover, just to prove that riddle No. 1 is all wrong.

Questionnaire

If the house next door went on fire, would you?:

a Laugh and phone all your friends to come and watch.

b Submerge yourself in a bathful of water.

c Call the fire brigade.

If your cat got stuck up a tree would you?:

a Cut the tree down.

b Get another cat.

c Call the fire brigade.

If you see a boy with his head trapped in some railings would you?:

a Call him bighead, but tell him you know of a good head shrinker.

b Throw rotten tomatoes at him.

c Call the fire brigade.

Stage Nerve

"Oh – it's just a stage he's going through!"

The Inseparable Families

A method of arranging cards in groups so that they cannot be separated.

Take the King, Queen, and Jack of each suit, and lay them out with every appearance of carelessness, but in accordance with the following rules.

The first row must be all of different suits; the second row must commence with a card similar in suit to the last card of the first row, and the following three cards must be respectively of the same suits as the first three cards in the first row. The third row is arranged exactly as the second in principle, referring, however, to that row immediately above it as to the suits of the cards. As an example look at the following:

Diamond	Club	Heart	Spade
Spade	Diamond	Club	Heart
Heart	Spade	Diamond	Club

Having laid out the cards in this manner pick them up again after some suitable patter, in vertical rows, beginning with the bottom card of the right-hand vertical row. If the cards are now dealt out into four heaps the King, Queen, and Jack of each suit will always be found together in one heap no matter how many times the cards may have been cut in the meantime. You should, of course, make a point of allowing the cards to be cut (not shuffled) after you have picked them up.

If one of your audience says he can see how it is done, try the following variation on him. Add the four Aces to the cards already used, and then lay them all out on this system. Place five cards in the first row making the cards at each end of the row of the same suit. Commence the second row with a card of the same suit as the fourth card in the first row; the second, third, fourth, and fifth cards of the row must be of the same suits respectively as the first, second, third, and fourth cards of the first row. Similarly with the third row, referring of course to the second rows as to the suit of the cards.

The odd card you have left you should place by itself below all the others. Here is an example:

Spade	Diamond	Heart	Club	Spade
Club	Spade	Diamond	Heart	Club
Heart	Club	Spade	Diamond	Club
		Diamond		

Pick the cards up, beginning with the odd card, and carrying on from the last card of the bottom row as before. If dealt out in four heaps after any amount of cutting the Ace, King, Queen, and Jack of one and the same suit will be found in each heap.

Pull the Other One

Ned picked up a hat from a puddle of mud
And found the head of his old friend Bud.
So across the mud he threw a plank,
Then grabbed Bud's collar and started to yank.
But Bud yelled, 'Ned, I'm all right! Let me be!
I've got a good horse down here under me!'

*

There's a man in Miami who walks so slow
He always wears spurs with sharp little wheels.
He says he wears them to keep his shadow
From stepping on his heels.

His younger sister lives so fast
She's now a year older than her brother.
In fact, if she can manage to last,
She'll soon be as old as her mother.

*

If you feed a hen on sawdust,
It's almost sure to wreck her,
And if she hatches one of her eggs,
Out will come a woodpecker.

*

Thing No. 13

SPOT THE DIFFERENCE

The two pictures above are not the same.
In the second picture the artist has made 28 changes. Can you spot them?

Here is a clue:
You should be able to SPOT them quite easily.

Here is another clue:
If you can't SPOT the difference you must be DOTTY!

And here is another clue:
The man on the right has 28 dots on his face, but the man on the left hasn't.

I'm not giving any more clues – I don't want to make it *too* easy.

Word Squares

Try to find words in these letter puzzles.

For example: DYE, YES, PRAY, RAY, NO, HIS, IS, HISS

S	P	N	H
L	R	O	I
O	A	O	S
D	Y	E	S

F	L	O	P	I	G
M	R	K	A	P	L
T	I	N	S	E	L
C	M	O	S	T	A
L	P	C	U	P	W
T	K	K	Z	O	O

P	A	C	U	K	T
E	A	S	T	E	R
L	I	K	E	E	U
T	R	I	N	P	S
I	F	P	T	O	T
P	R	O	P	C	S

Balancing Feats

Ask someone to stand sideways against a wall with his feet together and his right shoulder and the right side of his right foot touching the wall. Now tell him to lift his left leg. He will find it impossible.

Get someone to stand with his back to the wall, his feet together and touching the wall. Then put a ten pence piece on the floor a little way in front of his feet, and tell him he can have it if he can bend down, pick it up, and return to his original position, with his heels touching the wall the whole time. This, too, is impossible.

Tying a Cigarette in a Knot

Can you tie a cigarette in a knot without breaking it? It's easy. Simply roll it in cellophane (take it from the outside wrapper of the cigarette packet) twist the ends securely and you will find that the cigarette can be tied in a knot. When it is opened out, although a little bedraggled, it is still quite 'smokeable'.

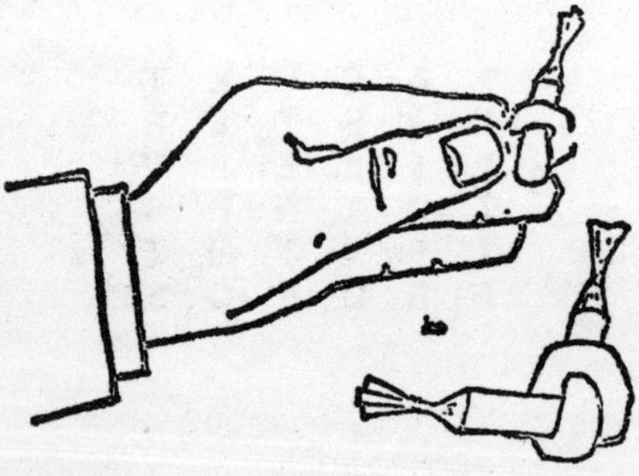

Nonsense Facts

Did you know that if you laid a mile of pennies in a straight line they'd add up to a very sore back?

Do you know why elephants never forget?
No one ever tells them anything.

Do you know that if you drink a pint of whitewash after every meal you'll never have to clean your teeth.

Did you know that the best shoes are made of leather, but banana skins make the best slippers?

Do you know that if a snail walked up your arm it would be a fortnight before you yelped, 'Oh, that's tickly!'

Do you know how to tell the hottest day of the year?
It's when you see a dog chasing a cat and they're both walking.

Do you know that the best way to get fresh hard-boiled eggs is to keep your hens in a hot house.

Do you know that if you feed grape vines with hair tonic you get a crop of gooseberries.

Thing No. 14

A TRICK WITH STRING

Can you pick up a piece of string, with one end in each hand – and tie a knot in it WITHOUT LETTING GO OF THE STRING?

Here's how you do it:

Before you pick up the string, fold your arms;

Next, with your arms still folded, pick up the string:

Unfold your arms, holding tight to the string – And you will find there is a knot in it!

Pair the Words

See if you can pair the words on the left with words on the right. For example, kneecap.

Knee	Weight
Hair	Radish
Sugar	Cushion
Book	Cap
Shoe	Tongs
Block	Mark
Cob	Hammer
Paper	Apple
Brief	Well
Horse	Board
Pine	Brush
Engagement	Tree
Soap	Web
Black	Ring
Pin	Case
Ink	Dish

How to Make a Kite

Materials: Thin cane, string, coloured paper, glue, scissors, coloured material.

To make the framework of the kite cut two lengths of cane. One should be twice as long as the other. Use a knife to make a groove at either end of the rods and bore a hole just below it. Cross these rods so that the distances OA, OB, and OC are equal. Then run a piece of string through the grooves, keeping it taut. Knot the ends of the string together.

Place the frame on a sheet of coloured paper. Cut the paper as shown, fold it, and glue over the cane.

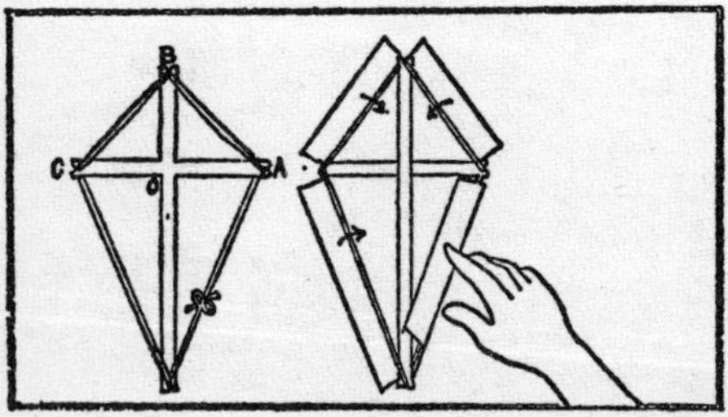

Carefully make two holes in the paper at the point where you made holes in the rods. Thread some thin string through them as shown below. Try to keep the distances AC, AD and AB equal.

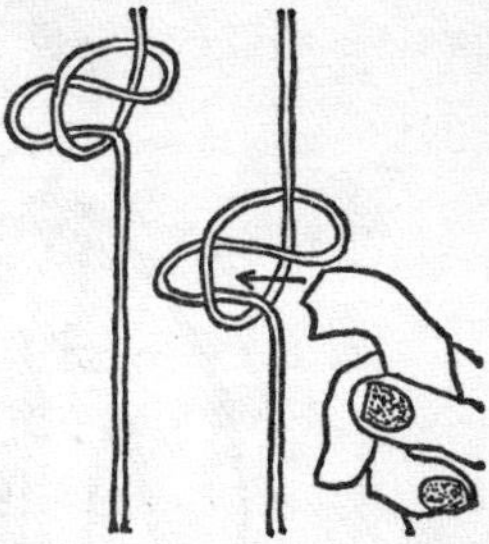

Perhaps the most attractive part of a kite is the tail.

You can make it by tying pieces of coloured material to a piece of string attached to the bottom of the kite. This is shown in the picture.

Finish the tail with a tassel of strips of coloured material.

Thing No. 15

FIRST AID HINT

WRONG!

Matchbox Puzzles

Here's a trick that will startle your friends. Producing an ordinary matchbox from your pocket, ask your friends whether they would like to look inside. They will be amazed when they see, carefully laid on cotton-wool, part of a finger.

Here's how it's done. Your friends do not know that the finger is really one of your own inserted through a hole in the bottom of the box.

Cut the underneath of the cover as shown in the sketch, so that you can slide it on and off with your finger still in position.

Empty Full

Bring a matchbox from your pocket and open it. It is empty. Hey presto! Open it again and it is full of matches. Of course the box is prepared. It has a partition across the middle and one half of the tray is empty but the other half contains matches cut in two as shown in the sketch.

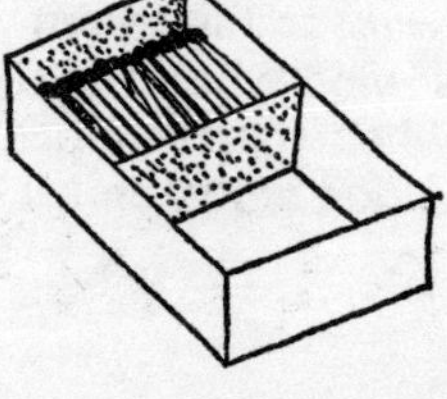

Old Mother Hubbard and Her Dog

Sarah Catherine Martin

Old Mother Hubbard
Went to the cupboard,
To fetch her poor dog a bone;
But when she got there
The cupboard was bare,
And so the poor dog had none.

She went to the baker's
To buy him some bread;
But when she came back
The poor dog was dead.

She went to the undertaker's
To buy him a coffin;
But when she came back
The poor dog was laughin'.

She took a clean dish
To get him some tripe;
But when she came back
He was smoking a pipe.

She went to the alehouse
To get him some beer;
But when she came back
The dog sat in a chair.

She went to the tavern
For wine white and red;
But when she came back
The dog stood on his head.

She went to the fruiterer's
  To buy him some fruit;
But when she came back
  He was playing the flute.

She went to the tailor's
  To buy him a coat;
But when she came back
  He was riding a goat.

She went to the hatter's,
  To buy him a hat;
But when she came back
  He was feeding the cat.

She went to the barber's
  To buy him a wig;
But when she came back
  He was dancing a jig.

She went to the cobbler's
  To buy him some shoes;
But when she came back
  He was reading the news.

She went to the seamstress
  To buy him some linen;
But when she came back
  The dog was a-spinnin'.

She went to the hosier's
  To buy him some hose;
But when she came back
  He was dressed in his clothes.

The dame made a curtsy,
  The dog made a bow;
The dame said: 'Your servant.'
  The dog said: 'Bow-wow!'

More Doodles

A pillar box seen from the inside

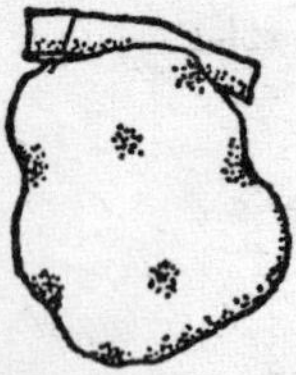

A potato with a chip on its shoulder

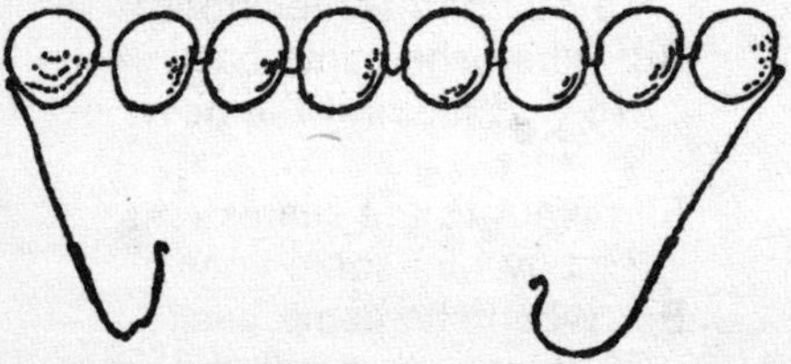

A communal spectacle for four people

A pig hiding behind a fence

A black eye

Thing No. 16

A NICE HOBBY

How to Make a Ship in a Bottle

You will need:

I of these;

and lots of bits of:

String
Wood
Paper
Pins

and: A sharp knife
A saw
Some glue

and also: A book of instructions. (I had one once but I lost it. I know it was something to do with a bottle, and a ship which you make from all those bits and pieces. Anyway, I had to do it from memory, but I'm quite pleased with the result. I've got it standing on the mantelpiece and a lot of people look at it, and some people admire it, but not all of them).

Here is a picture of it. Perhaps it's not *exactly* right. See what you think. And if you do happen to find a book of instructions, please write and let me know where I went wrong.

Snake Story

Two snakes found an egg and started quarrelling over it. Somehow each got hold of the other's tail and began to swallow. They swallowed and swallowed until at last there was nothing at all left except the egg over which they had quarrelled.

Tying Up the Stones

A countryman who had never been in a city or seen a paved street came to London. He was walking along when suddenly a dog came out of a house and ran furiously at him. The man stooped down to pick up a stone to throw at the dog, but found all the stones fixed tight in the cobble-stone paving. 'What a strange country I am in,' said the man, 'where the people tie up the stones and let the dogs loose.'

Dice Puzzle

= 10

= 13

WHAT DOES  EQUAL

More Riddles

What's the best way to feel better off?
Sit on a hot stove.

Which has the more legs, one horse or no horse?
No horse, because no horse has 5 legs!

What is nothing?
A bottomless bucket without any sides.

What always walks on its head?
A nail in a shoe.

What rises, falls, wears out boots yet cannot walk?
A football.

Which is the left side of a pudding?
The side that is not eaten.

What horse never bites?
A clothes horse.

What is always top of the class?
The ceiling.

When is soup likely to run out of the pot?
When there's a leek in it.

What are the best book markers?
Dirty fingers.

What's Going On?

Tommy and Peter went to the cinema, and this is what they saw. But so many things happened in such a short time that they couldn't agree afterwards what had taken place. Can you help them? Look carefully at the picture for 30 seconds, cover it up, and then answer the following questions! No cheating!

1. Where was the stage-coach going?
2. How many passengers sat in it?
3. What were they doing?
4. Where was the driver?
5. What did the Indian hit with his arrow?
6. Who fired the gun and what did he hit?
7. What was the weather like?
8. How much luggage was on the stage-coach?

Yet More Astounding Facts

Prison Break

With iron-jawed determination a convict forced his way out of a German gaol in 1907 by a method that is likely to remain unique among prison escapes. The cell in which robber Hans Schaarschmidt was locked up in the somewhat antiquated gaol at Gera was barred at the window, not with iron but with two oak beams – a crosspiece 7 in. thick, and outside that a vertical piece 9 in. thick. Fed mostly on black bread and with plenty of time before him – he had a six-year sentence to serve – Schaarschmidt began to chew the beam with his teeth. He replaced the wood he gnawed away with a growing mass of black bread paste. In three months he got through the inner beam, in four more the outer. Then he wriggled out, at the cost of severe lacerations. Unfortunately, this prodigious accomplishment earned him only three weeks of liberty. He was recaptured, heartlessly brought back with teeth much worn down and jaws mightily muscled, and placed in another cell – with iron bars.

Brief Notes

The shortest correspondence on record was an example of brevity in letter writing that would be hard to surpass. Victor Hugo, away on a well-earned holiday in 1862 but anxious to hear how his new novel was selling, wrote to his publisher: '?' Back came the exultant answer: '!' Oddly, the book in question was *Les Miserables*, filling 1,995 pages of print – one of the longest novels of all time.

Make a Pair

Can you pair the pictures?

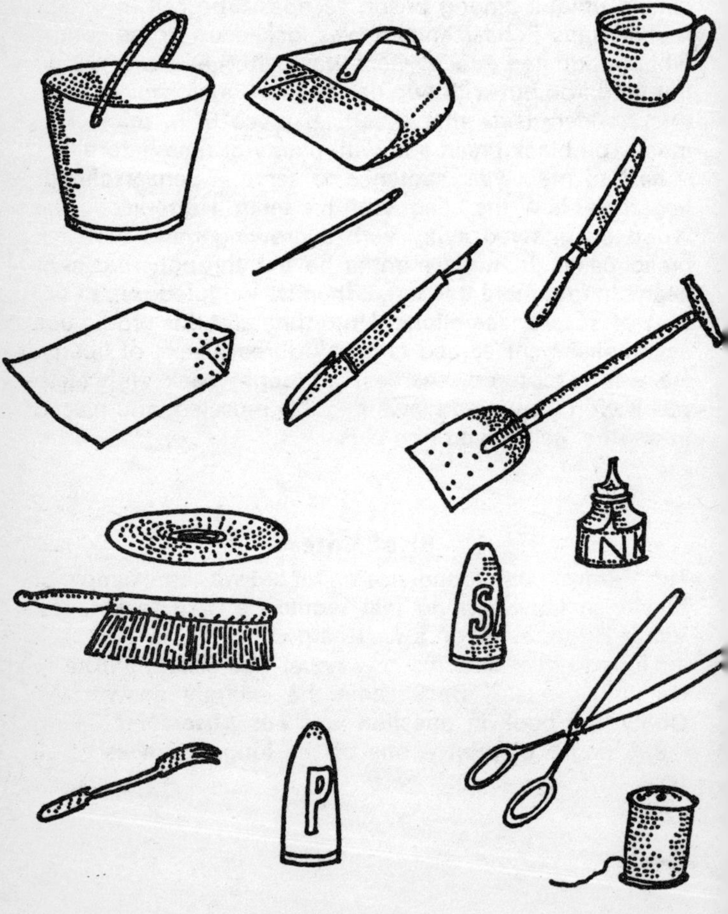

Thing No. 17

NATURE HINT

How to tell the difference between a weasel and a stoat.

Of course, everybody knows that a weasel is weasely distinguished. And a stoat? Well, that's stoatally different.

But that is not a very scientific answer. No – this is how you do it if you are a proper naturalist:

Listen carefully.
If you can't hear anything
it's probably a stoat.
Weasels go 'Pop'.

Fun With Numbers

This figure trick will give you an opportunity to indulge in a little leg-pulling at the expense of one of your friends. Ask him to come to the blackboard and write down the figures 1—9, omitting the figure 8. Now ask the others which figure they consider to be the least well written. This number is to be multiplied by 9 and the product is to be used to multiply the whole row of figures 1–9, excluding 8.

An example will make this clear. Assuming that the badly written number is 5, when multiplied by 9 the result is 45 and when, 1 2 3 4 5 6 7 9 is multiplied by 45 the answer is 555555555.

When your friend reaches the stage of writing the answer you can raise a laugh by remarking that you hope the practice will ensure that he writes the figure more legibly in future. No matter what figure is decided upon as the least well written, the final answer to the sum will be a row of that figure if the instructions are carefully followed.

For example:

```
  12345679
      ×45
 ----------
  61728395
+493827160
 ----------
 555555555
 ----------
```

Good for a Laugh

'What was the name of that hotel we stayed at dear?'

'Just a moment, luv. I'll run upstairs and look through the towels.'

FOR SALE

Baker's Business, good trade, large oven. Owner has been in it for many years.

And as one miser said to another on being shipwrecked, 'It's a good thing we didn't buy return tickets.'

Papa Bear: 'Somebody's been eating my porridge.'

Baby Bear: 'And somebody's been eating my porridge.'

Mother Bear: 'Shut up, you idiots. I haven't served it yet.'

Mr Yates, headmaster of the village school retired last week. His pupils joined together to give him a little momentum.

A visitor to a lunatic asylum was accosted by an inmate. The latter cupped his hands and said to the visitor:

'Guess what I have here?' The visitor, trying to be agreeable, said, 'Ten thousand pounds.'

'No,' replied the inmate, chuckling because the answer was wrong.

'Guess again.'

'Well, er – let me see. A live dog.'

'No,' the inmate replied once more. 'Guess again.'

'A motor bus.'

'No.'

'A row of houses, then?'

The inmate opened his two hands ever so slightly and peered inside them. Then looking up, he demanded, 'How many houses?'

Find the Truants

The class is having a photograph taken with the teacher in the middle of the front row. He looks quite happy, but he wouldn't look so happy if he knew that two of his pupils are hiding. He didn't discover this until he'd received the photograph. Can you find the two missing pupils?

More Limericks

An unpopular youth from Cologne
With a pain in his tummy did mogne.
He heaved a great sigh
And said, 'I would digh,
But the loss would be only my own.'

There was a young fellow from Crewe.
Who decided to build a canoe.
When out on the river
He found with a shiver
That he hadn't used waterproof glue.

Not Always Skin Deep

'*Mummie!*' said little Johnny one day at the zoo. 'Doesn't that baboon look just like Uncle Lew?'

'*Sh! Child!*' said mother and slapped him on the hand.

'Why, Mummie, the baboon doesn't understand!'

One Is Right

Here are six different ways an Eight of Clubs might be drawn. Yet, there is a standard way of doing it, as you would discover by examining any deck of cards. Which one is right?

How to Name Four Cards Cut by a Member of the Audience

This is a particularly good trick and depends primarily on getting sight of the top card. It must be carried out rapidly and without hesitation, however, as success depends absolutely on bluff.

Offer the pack to be shuffled by the audience; take it back after this has been done, and while pattering, contrive to find out what is the top card. Next ask a member of the audience to cut the pack three times so as to leave four packets in a row on the table. The last packet he puts down will have as its top card the top card of the pack, which you know and we will suppose to be the Queen of Hearts. Now placing your hand on the top of the packet *farthest* from that on which is the Queen of Hearts, *you pick it up but do not show it to the audience.* Instead you quickly note what it is and immediately announce it as the top card of the next packet, which card you thereupon pick up. You repeat this bluff with the remaining two top cards allowing no pause. As you pick the cards up you arrange them fan-wise in your left hand, taking care that the last card picked up (the Queen of Hearts) is placed as the first card of the fan. Then you turn them all towards the audience, and they find that the four cards you have named are actually in your hand. They will invariably attribute the trick to some marvellous sleight on your part.

Bear in mind, however, that success depends on easy rapidity.

Thing No. 18

A GARDEN IN A BOTTLE

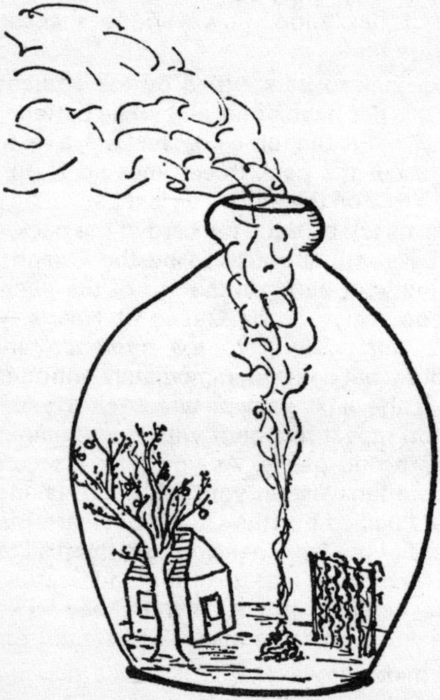

You need a big bottle.

Grow things in the bottle.

(I think the bonfire was a mistake. It might get out of hand and burn the shed down or something.)

Hidden Birds

In the jumbled words below you will find some hidden birds.
Do you know what they are?

How to Make a Lantern

Materials: White paper, scissors, glue, compasses.

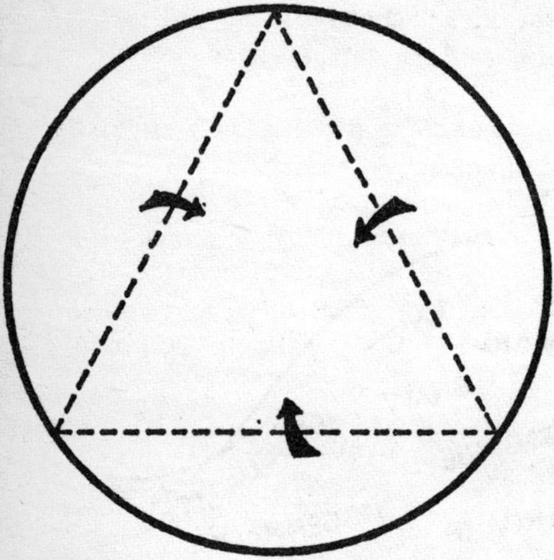

Cut out twenty circles, the same size as the one shown here.

Fold each circle upwards on the dotted lines.

You now have twent shapes like this.

Stick them together b joining the sides so tha you have five triangle meeting at each corner

The Laughing Policeman

A detective in a West End store pointed out a woman customer to his friend.

'Do you see that woman ?' he asked. 'Well she's suffering from kleptomania,' the detective confided.

'Good gracious ! Why doesn't she take something for it ?'

'She will in a minute,' said the detective.

Fred : 'Stealing that slice of gateaux was easy, wasn't it ?'
Bill : 'Yeah ; a piece of cake.'

Defendant : 'No, your honour, I was not drunk, but merely under the influence of alcohol.'
Judge : 'In that case, instead of sentencing you to fourteen days in prison, I'll send you there for two weeks.'

What do policemen put in their sandwiches ?
Truncheon meat.

Judge : 'You are a bus conductor and you have been accused of witchcraft. What have you got to say to that ?'
Bus Conductor : 'Well, we reached the bus terminus and I shouted "All change" and when I looked, I had a bus full of frogs.'

Recruits to the police force must have big feet because they can cover more ground on their beat.

Did you know that two feet make one Scotland yard.

Did you hear about the policeman who when he was off duty started to play the drums ?
He liked being on the beat.

Thing No. 19

HOW TO CATCH A BURGLAR

Hung Up

There are eight differences between these two pictures. Can you get them all?

Two Coin Puzzles

Try these coin puzzles on some friends.

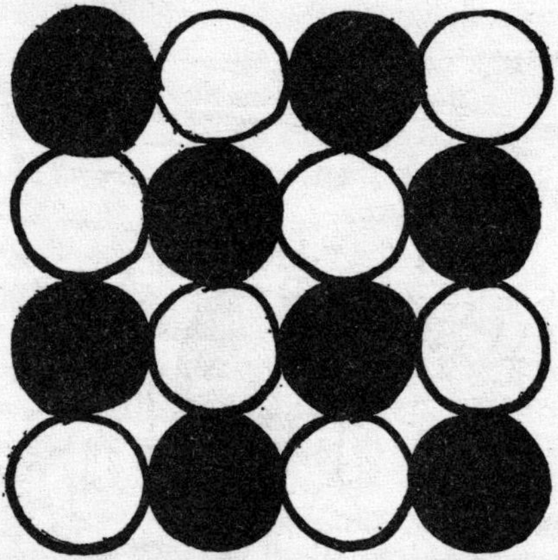

1. Arrange sixteen identical coins as illustrated. Black is heads, white tails. Touching only two of the coins, arrange them so vertical rows are either all heads or all tails. There'll be two of each.

2. Have friends put any number of coins on the table they wish. Without looking, say you can make the quantity change so an odd number becomes even, or an even number becomes odd. Then prove it.

Thing No. 20

METEOROLOGY

A meteorologist is a man who can
tell whether.
Whether it's going to rain.
Whether it's going to be fine.
Whether it's going to be unsettled
for a time and then break out in
all sorts of things.

Some people say that meteorologists are very clever people because when they say it's going to be a lovely day with temperatures in the eighties and not a cloud in the sky, they always have to be able to tell you – the following day – what caused the snow and ice and hail and rain and sleet and drizzle.

Of course, it's very easy to mock at meteorologists. Try it.

See how easy it is?

But they really do have to do a lot of studying and they have to know lots of things that most of us have never even heard of.

These are just a few of the subjects a meteorologist has to study:

Rainology
Sea-weedology
Corn-on-the-big-toe-ology

They also have to use enormous charts and maps which are very difficult to carry backwards and forwards to their offices. For this reason they must be qualified cartographers. In case a wheel comes off, I suppose.

Now you know how clever they are, I hope you try to change your attitude.

The next time the weather-man on television tells you it's going to be a lovely day – trust him.

Have a little faith.

Go out in the country, arrange a nice picnic, forget your worries.

PS. Don't forget your umbrella.

Pull the Other One

A lady fell into the sea
And up from the deep and dark
Came an ugly fin, but luckily
It was a *man*-eating shark!

Sally is so extremely modest
She always wears glasses – and why?
To keep her from looking at anything
With her naked eye.

They say that Billy Earthquake,
Who had his run-ins with the law,
Could stand in front of a mirror
And beat himself to the draw.

There's a man so tall in Colorado
That when he wants to shave
He has to climb to the top of a ladder.
They call him Daring Dave.

From the burning house their dog
Brought little Nance and Lee,
Then went back in and fetched the fire
Insurance policy!

More Picture Puns

Can you guess from the picture what the words are?

Thing No. 21

FIRST AID HINT

1. Treat the patient for flat feet.

2. Continue the treatment all over.

Riddiculous

What kind of sweet goes swinging through the jungle?
Tarzipan.

What leaves yellow footprints in the sea bed?
A lemon sole.

What lies on the ground a hundred feet up in the air?
A centipede lying on its back.

What can fall on water without getting wet?
A shadow.

What carries lots of people and lives under the sea?
An octobus.

When is an artist dangerous?
When he draws a gun.

What kind of servants are best for hotels?
The inn-experienced.

Who is the oldest settler in the West?
The sun.

How many feet has a horse?
Six. Forefeet in front and two behind.

What is the difference between a big hill and a big pill?
One is hard to go up and the other is hard to get down.

Who was the fastest runner in the world?
Adam. He was the first in the human race.

A Fate Better Than Death

Tried and condemned to death for a brutal murder, John Lee mounted the scaffold in a British prison yard. Then fate – or something – inexplicably interceded for John Lee in a way that would have been incredible if it hadn't been witnessed three-quarters of a century ago by awed officials and newspaper men. After standing Lee on the trap door and adjusting the noose the sheriff stepped away and signalled. The bolt was withdrawn, but the door did not fall. They moved Lee off it and made a test; the door dropped as it should. With Lee back in place, they drew the bolt again; the door stayed level. Lee was returned to his cell while anxious warders determined by inspection that the bolt and hinges were in perfect working order. To make sure the door couldn't jam, they brought a plane and shaved the edges. For a final test a warder stood in position, clutching the rope; when the bolt was drawn the door dropped him instantly. But when John Lee was brought back to stand on it the door twice again refused to budge. The distraught sheriff gave up and telegraphed the Home Secretary. Newspapers trumpeted the story sensationally. Parliament debated the matter and denounced irresponsible talk of witchcraft before agreeing to commute Lee's sentence to a life term. The case of the man who couldn't be hanged was never solved, and in view of the circumstances, friendless, penniless John Lee had no means to bribe officials, who plainly did their best to hang him. It remains one of the uncanniest mysteries of modern times.

Thing No. 22

ETIQUETTE

A gentleman should always offer his seat to a lady.

Inspector Markham Investigates

Can you solve the crime?

Queer Places

Here are some really strange American county names:

MURDERVILLE
TOMBSTONE
ROARING FOX
THIEF'S END
STARVATION
HIDE AND SEEK
BUGSVILLE
JACKPOT
SKELETONVILLE
FIGHTING COCKS
STICKUP CANYON
BLUDGEONVILLE
LAUGHTER'S LOSS

Where Are You?

Here are some British towns shown in pictures. Do you know what they are?

A Little Basic

Mama Skunk was worried because she could never keep track of her two children. They were named In and Out, and whenever In was in, Out was out, and if Out was in, In was out.

One day she called Out in to her and told him to go out and bring In in. So out Out went, and in no time at all he brought In in.

'Wonderful,' said Mama Skunk, 'how in all that great forest could you find In in so short a time?'

And out replied, 'In stinct!'

Turtle Tattle

Two large turtles and a small turtle went into an ice-cream parlour and ordered three delicious sundaes. While they were waiting for their ice-cream, they noticed it had started to rain.

'We're going to need our umbrella,' said one big turtle, and the other big one agreed. The two of them decided that the little turtle should run home and get it. But the little turtle didn't want to go because he was afraid the two big turtles would eat his sundae. However, they promised not to, and finally the little turtle started off.

A week went by, then two weeks. At the end of the third week one of the big turtles turned to the other and said, 'Oh come on, let's eat his ice-cream sundae.'

'All right,' agreed his companion.

'If you do, I won't go for that umbrella,' cried the little turtle, sticking his head out from under the counter at the other end of the shop.

Christmas Pudding

Cook is very pleased with his delicious Christmas Pudding. Do you know what the ingredients are?

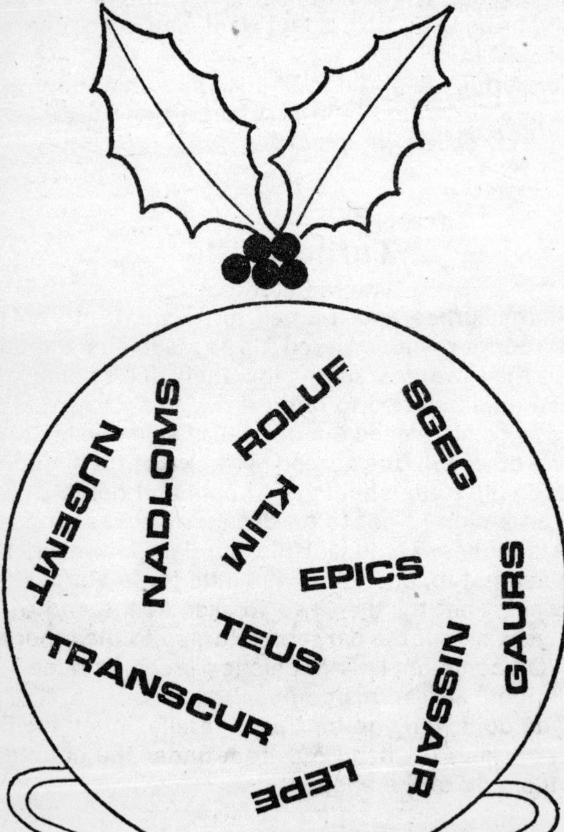

Strange Types

'The radiator leaks.'

A Triangular Puzzle

Make this single triangle into 4 triangles by adding 3 straight lines of equal length.

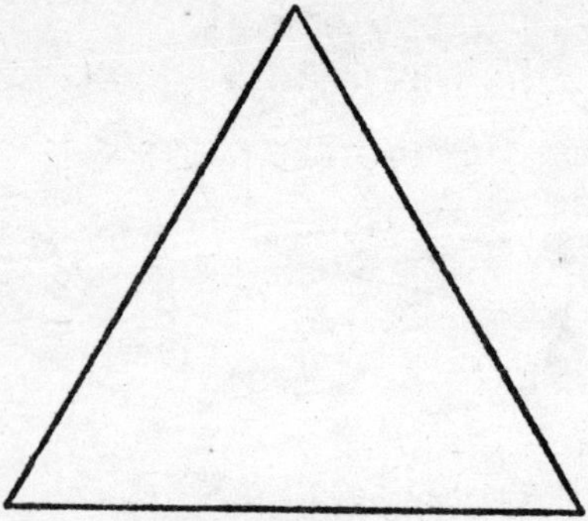

The Penny and the Piece of Paper

Take a twopenny piece and a piece of paper cut into the same shape as the coin. Let these two bodies fall at the same moment side by side. You will find that the coin will reach the ground a long while before the disc of paper. But now place the piece of paper upon the upper surface of the two pence, and with your finger firmly pressing the paper to the coin, let them fall together in a horizontal position. You will find that the two bodies will reach the ground at the same time!

Why?

The piece of paper is protected from the action of the air by the coin. The weight of the bodies counts for nothing in their fall. It is the air only which prevents them from falling with the same velocity.

Test Your Memory

Here's a puzzle which you can use to test your own – and your pal's – memory. Look carefully at the picture for one minute, then place a piece of paper over it and answer the questions below.

1. Where's the train going to?
2. What time is it by the station clock?
3. What's on the porter's barrow?
4. What kind of animals are on the train?
5. What has fallen out of the delayed passenger's case?

Thing No. 23

PICTURE QUIZ

Question:

What does this horrible picture become if you turn it upside down?

Answer:

Worse.

Contradict Me If I'm Wrong

'Twas midnight on the ocean,
Not a streetcar was in sight;
The sun was shining brightly,
For it rained all day that night.
'Twas a summer's day in winter
The snow was raining fast,
As a barefoot girl with shoes on
Stood sitting on the grass.
'Twas evening and the rising sun
Was setting in the west;
And all the fishes in the trees
Were curled up in their nests.
The rain was pouring down,
The sun was shining bright,
And 'twas midday on the ocean
In the middle of the night.

Anon.

Batty

Two bats, hanging upside down, were watching another bat acting in a rather strange way.

'He's behaving very queer,' said the first bat.

'Oh, don't mind him,' replied the second. 'He's got men in the belfry.'

Riddles Galore

Why is a fishmonger never a good husband?

Because his customers make him sellfish.

Why is a horse in the act of jumping a fence like a penny?

Because he has a head on one side and a tail on the other.

Why do people say that Moses wore a wig?

Because he sometimes appeared with Aaron and sometimes without 'air on!

What is better than presence of mind in a railway accident?

Absence of body.

Why is it hard for a leopard to hide in the jungle?

Because he's always spotted.

What did the ground say to the rain?

If you keep this up my name will be mud.

What is the difference between a comma and a tiger?

One has a pause at the end of its clause, and the other has claws at the ends of its paws.

What became of the man who stole the calendar?

He got twelve months.

OO?

The following words all have double O in them. Do you know what they are?

An ape	---OO-
A great din	--------OO
To turn upwards suddenly at a sharp angle	-OO-
A form of black magic	-OO-OO
Unfastened	-OO--
A rigged vessel with one mast	--OO-
Recklessly bold	-OO------
A violent hurricane	----OO-
An Australian curved weapon	-OO------
Shipwrecked	---OO---
A bird that rejects its young	----OO

Many-legs

Tom: 'It must be painful when a giraffe has a sore throat.'

Tim: 'Imagine a whale with lock jaw, or a hippopotamus with chapped lips!'

Tom: 'How about a shark with toothache?'

Tim: 'Or an African elephant with earache.'

Tom: 'I'm going to sit down. My feet hurt.'

Tim: 'You should be glad you're not one of those!'

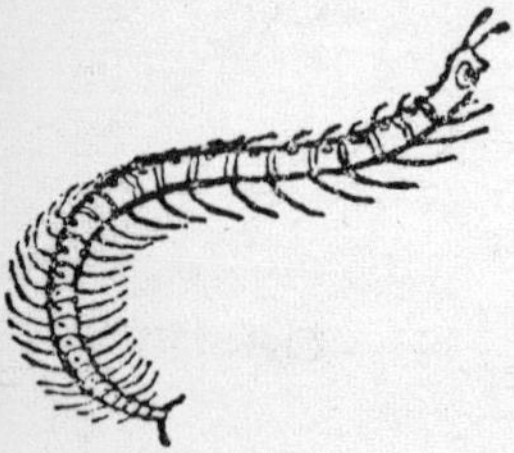

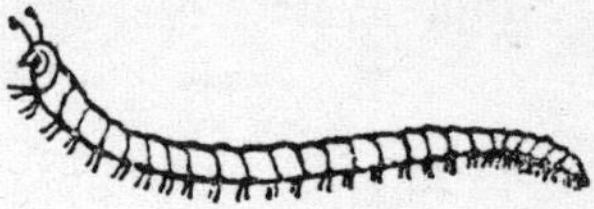

The Centipede

A. P. Herbert

The centipede is not quite nice;
He lives in idleness and vice;
He has a hundred legs.
He also has a hundred wives,
And each of these if she survives
Has just a hundred eggs;
So that's the reason if you pick
Up any boulder, stone or brick
You nearly always find
A swarm of centipedes concealed;
They scatter far across the field,
But *one* remains behind.

The Centipede

And you may reckon then, my son,
That not alone that luckless one
Lies pitiful and torn,
But millions more of either sex—
100 multiplied by X—
Will never now be born;
I dare say it will make you sick,
But so does all Arithmetic.

The gardener says, I ought to add,
The centipede is not so bad;
He rather likes the brutes.
The millipede is what he loathes;
He uses wild bucolic oaths
Because it eats his roots;
And every gardener is agreed
That if you see a centipede
Conversing with a milli—
On one of them you drop a stone,
The other one you leave alone—
I think that's rather silly;
They may be right, but what I say
Is 'Can one stand about all day
And *count* the creature's legs?'
It has too many any way,
And any moment it may lay
Another hundred eggs!
So if I see a thing like *this*
I murmur 'Without prejudice',
And knock it on the head;
And if I see a thing like *that*
I take a brick and squash it flat;
In either case it's dead.

Thing No. 24

A PICTURE QUIZ

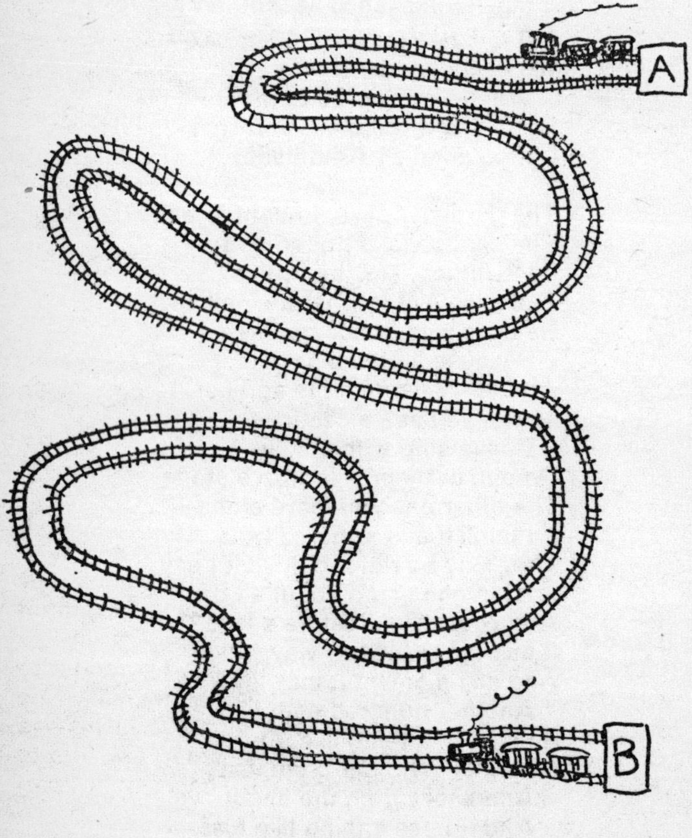

It takes 2 hours to travel between A and B.
In the picture above you can see one train leaving A and another leaving B.
The time is 3 p.m.
At what time will these two trains pass each other?

Engraved Eggs

Write your name, or draw a pattern on the eggshell with beeswax, varnish, or even tallow. Plunge the egg into vinegar. Wherever the shell is not protected by the covering material it is decomposed and the design stands out in relief.

It takes 2 to 3 hours to bring out the tracing. You can use eggs that have been blown, but they will have to be weighted or held down in the vinegar.

On all plain post cards is printed a sentence beneath the words 'Post Card'. What is it?

Answer:

'The address to be written on this side'.

Matchless

Throw 5 matches on the table and ask someone if they can arrange the matches to form the number 19 without breaking or bending the matches.

Well, perhaps there will be an extra smart person who will tumble to the solution before you show him. If he does, you can still get even with him. When he has arranged the matches in the correct order, ask him to remove 1 and make the number 20. That should completely fox him.

The solution is to take the centre match away and this will leave the Roman numeral for 20.

XIX

XX

The cheetah, my dearest, is known not to cheat

George Barker

The cheetah, my dearest, is known not to cheat;
the Tiger possesses no tie;
The horse-fly, of course, was never a horse;
the lion will not tell a lie.

The turkey, though perky, was never a Turk;
nor the monkey ever a monk;
the mandrel, though like one, was never a man,
but some men are like him, when drunk.

The springbok, dear thing, was not born in the Spring;
The walrus will not build a wall.
No badger is bad; no adder can add.
There is no truth in these things at all.

toucannery

Jack Prelutsky

whatever one toucan can do
is sooner done by toucans two
three toucans it's very true
can do much more than two can do

and toucans numbering two plus two can
manage more than all the zoo can
in fact there is no toucan who can
do what four or three or two can.

Down Tools

Here you have to find out how many people were in the house and the garden, before they all ran out to buy an ice-cream. They have each left what they were using. How many were there?

Crooked Smile

'You'd better make an appointment with the eye specialist, mate.'

Drunk and Disorderly

Two drunks were sitting on a train. One said to the other, as the train pulled into the station:

'Is this Wembley?'

'No, Thursday,' came the reply.

'So am I,' said the first drunk. 'Let's get out and have one.'

Convict to warden: 'I think my nose is going to start bleeding. Could you put your keys down my neck, please?'

Why did the thief carry a laundry bag?

He wanted to make a clean getaway.

Two drunks were playing with a flashlight, switching it on and off. Finally one of them threw a beam of light towards the ceiling and said, 'I bet you can't climb up that beam?' The other shook his head and said, 'No, siree, you can't get me to try that. I know you! Just when I get to the top you'll turn it off.'

Policeman: 'Stop! Where have I seen your face before?'

Thief: 'Same place as you see it now, mate!'

Burglar: 'Quick, jump out of the window. The police are coming!'

Accomplice: 'But we're on the thirteenth floor.'

Burglar: 'This is no time for superstition.'

Limericks

Edward Lear

There was an Old Man of the North,
Who fell into a basin of broth;
  But a laudable cook
  Fished him out with a hook,
Which saved that Old Man of the North.

There was an Old Person of Buda,
Whose conduct grew ruder and ruder,
  Till at last with a hammer
  They silenced his clamour,
By smashing that Person of Buda.

Observation Page

Here are twelve objects. Study them carefully for one minute, then list those you can remember. No cheatin g!

A Moving Puzzle

The following words have some kind of movement hidden in them. For example, in CRUNCH you will find the word RUN. Can you work out the rest?

CLEANLINESS
COWSLIP
SHOPPER
RETURNING
PARASITE

Parts of the Body

Now try this one. In these words parts of the body are hidden.

HARMLESS
DELIVERY
SHEARING
ALLEGIANCE
PLUNGE

Thing No. 25

QUIZ

A man looks at a photograph and says:
'Brothers and sisters have I none,
But this man's father is my father's son.'

Question 1

Whose photograph is he looking at?

Question 2

Why does he talk in riddles?

Question 3

Would you be content with a photograph that looks like a question-mark?

Question 4

Is that a mouse-trap on the table?
Huh?

Little Miss . . .

Little Miss Muffet,
Sat on a tuffet,
Eating her Irish stew.
Along came a spider
And sat down beside her
So she ate *him* up, too.

Anon.

Little Miss Tuckett
Sat on a bucket,
Eating some peaches and cream;
There came a grasshopper
And tried hard to stop her;
But she said, 'Go away, or I'll scream.'

A Match Poser

Study this drawing.

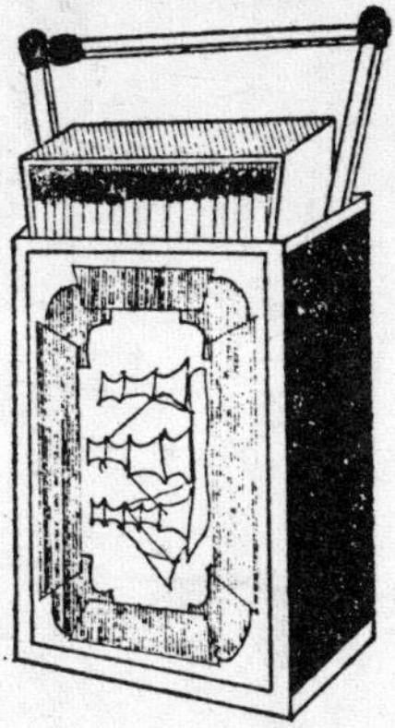

Now imagine a fourth match is lit, and held under the middle of the horizontal match. Can you reason which of the two supporting side matches will be fired first? The one on the right or on the left? Will it be the side where there is only one phosphoric end, or where there are two ends tipped with phosphorus?

Answer:

At none of these. The side matches would not ignite at all, because immediately the centre of the horizontal match is burned, the two side matches would spring back and throw off the third match, which would then fall to the ground and be extinguished.

Top of the Pops

The Cat and the Mat Puzzle

MAT-----
-MAT---
--MAT-
---MAT--
----MAT-
------MAT

Fill the blanks above with letters so as to make words, each of which with MAT in the position indicated.

Try this one with CAT.

CAT---
-CAT---
--CAT-
---CAT---
----CAT-
-----CAT--

Thing No. 26

WHAT TO DO IF A WASP LANDS ON THE END OF YOUR NOSE

1. DON'T PANIC.
2. Find a great big hammer or mallet and go 'bash, bash, bash, bash, bash' right on his head.
   (Look here, I know you may not like the idea; you can't bear the thought of harming a little creature like that. But if you don't—he might sting you; and, my goodness, that would be very painful!)

   If you can't find a great big hammer or mallet:
3. PANIC.

A Cut Ice Cube Remains Whole

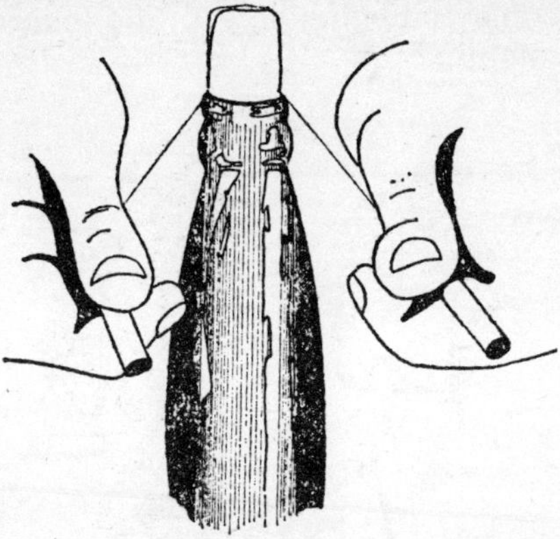

Would you believe you could cut through an ice cube without dividing it? The drawing above shows how to perform this feat.

Provide handles at the ends of an 8-inch length of thin wire by twisting each end around the middle of a pencil. Place an ice cube on top of a bottle. Then straddle the cube with the wire and bear down hard on the pencils.

Within a minute or so the wire will cut its way completely through the cube and come out the bottom. The ice cube, however, will still be whole and as solid as before you started!

How is this possible? Pressure causes the ice directly under the wire to melt. In melting, this ice steals heat from the ice surrounding it. The latter, colder ice refreezes the water after the wire has passed through.

Busy Bs

How many objects beginning with the letter **b** can you see in this picture?

My Father

Ted Hughes

Some fathers work at the office, others work at the
store,
Some operate great cranes and build up skyscrapers
galore,
Some work in canning factories counting green peas
into cans,
Some drive all night in huge and thundering removal
vans.
But mine has the strangest job of the lot.
My Father's the Chief Inspector of—What?
O don't tell the mice, don't tell the moles,
My Father's the Chief Inspector of HOLES.
It's a work of the highest importance because you
never know
What's in a hole, what fearful thing is creeping from
below.
Perhaps it's a hole to the ocean and will soon gush
water in tons,
Or maybe it leads to a vast cave full of gold and
skeletons.
Though a hole might seem to have nothing but dirt in,
Somebody's simply got to make certain.
Caves in the mountain, clefts in the wall,
My Father has to inspect them all.
That crack in the road looks harmless. My father knows
it's not.
The world may be breaking into two and starting at
that spot.
Or maybe the world is a great egg, and we live on the
shell,
And it's just beginning to split and hatch: you simply
cannot tell.

My Father

If you see a crack, run to the phone, run!
My Father will know just what's to be done.
A rumbling hole, a silent hole,
My Father will soon have it under control.
Keeping a check on all these holes he hurries from morning to night.
There might be sounds of marching in one, or an eye shining bright.
A tentacle came groping from a hole that belonged to a mouse,
A floor collapsed and Chinamen swarmed up into the house.
A Hole's an unpredictable thing—
Nobody knows what a Hole might bring.
Caves in the mountain, clefts in the wall,
My Father has to inspect them all!

Climb the Ladder

See if you can climb to the top of this four-letter word puzzle. Start at the bottom and change one letter of each word as you climb up.

Clues

1. To lure on by teasing.
2. Pleased.
3. Clothed.
4. To applaud.
5. Retractable nail of cat family.
6. Imperfection; fault.
7. An apartment; smooth.
8. A courageous deed.
9. Feeling of anxiety.
10. A fruit.
11. Lord of the realm; to look at closely.
12. Mooring place for ships.

Thing No. 27

SPOT THE BALL COMPETITION

At this very exciting moment an artist came along and rubbed out the ball. What a nasty thing to do.

Question: Can you find where the ball is?

Answer: Yes.

Question: How?

Answer: Take a pin and keep sticking it in the picture. Listen carefully. When you find the ball you will hear a noise something like 'Sssssssssssssssssssss'.

You must be joking!

You should never write secrets with a quill pen.
It might split.

Barber: 'I don't remember your face, sir.'
Customer: 'You wouldn't. It's healed up now.'

Passenger: 'How much to take me to the station?'
Cab driver: 'Fifty pence, sir. I'll take the bags for nothing.'
Passenger: 'Just take my bags then. I'll walk.'

'My brother's in the secret service.'
'Really? He must be clever.'
'I'll say he is. He's so smart, he's even got a code in the nose.'

A Scotsman sold a dog to an Englishman for £5 in spite of the fact that he had been offered £6 by an American. Reason?
The dog could walk back from London but could not swim across the Atlantic!

What's green, squishy and hairy and spends a lot of time under water?
A gooseberry with an aqua lung.

Bank Manager, giving identification after robbery: 'My missing cashier has a Roman nose.'
Policeman: 'We'll never catch him then. Roman noses never turn up.'

Coins in a Row

Here are six coins in two rows. Can you move one coin so that there are four coins in each row?

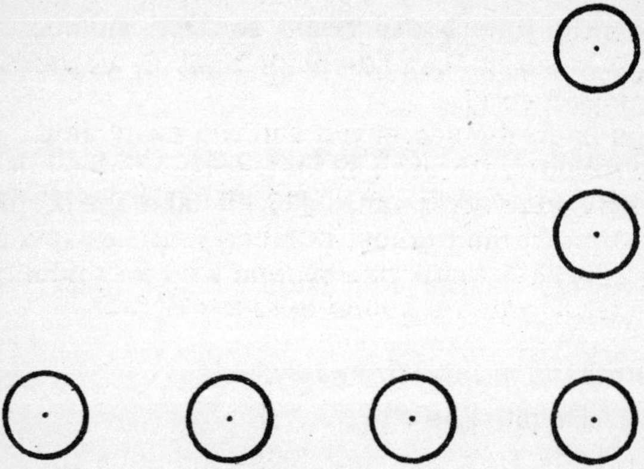

Optical Trick

Look at this triangle with eyes half-shut—and then with eyes wide open. The triangle will appear to project inward and then outward.

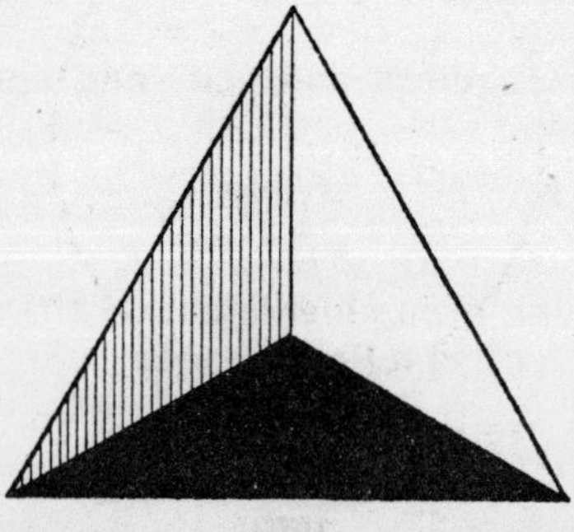

A Race Without Runners

Say to a friend: 'Let's have a race by numbers and see who can get to 99 first!' You can start at any number below 100 and the only rule is that you mustn't 'run' ahead by more than 9. For instance, if you say 17 to begin with, your friend could say any number from 18 to 26 inclusive, but he couldn't say 27 because that is 10 more than 17.

If you know the secret you can win every time.

Always strive to reach 89 first, and as far as possible always avoid multiples of 10 (10, 20, 30, 40, etc.). When you reach 89, the highest number your opponent can say next is 98 (9 more than 89) and whatever number he says after 89 you are bound to reach 99 first.

A Circular Puzzle

Can you divide the surface of this circle into four equal parts by drawing four curved lines?

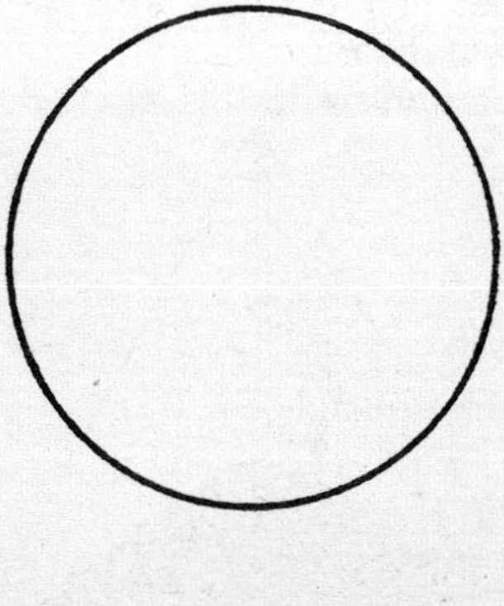

Knock Knock

'Knock Knock.'
'Who's there?'
'Con.'
'Con who?'
'Confidential—can't tell you.'

'Knock Knock.'
'Who's there?'
'Jo.'
'Jo who?'
'Jo always ask so many questions?'

'Knock Knock.'
'Who's there?'
'Linda.'
'Linda who?'
'Linda hand with this puncture.'

'Knock Knock.'
'Who's there?'
'Boo.'
'Boo who?'
'If you stop crying I'll tell you.'

The Modern Hiawatha

George A. Strong

He killed the noble Mudjokivis,
With the skin he made him mittens,
Made them with the fur side inside,
Made them with the skin side outside,
He, to get the warm side inside,
Put the inside skin side outside;
He, to get the cold side outside,
Put the warm side fur side inside.
That's why he put fur side inside,
Why he put the skin side outside,
Why he turned them inside outside.

A rabbit raced a turtle,
You know the turtle won;
And Mister Bunny came in late
A little hot cross bun.

Anon.

There once was a pilot named Heller
Who built a huge plane with propeller
But the thing never flew
For it wouldn't fit through,
The passage that led from his cellar.

Crazy Mixed-up Dogs

Here are some jumbled breeds of dogs. Can you work out what they are?

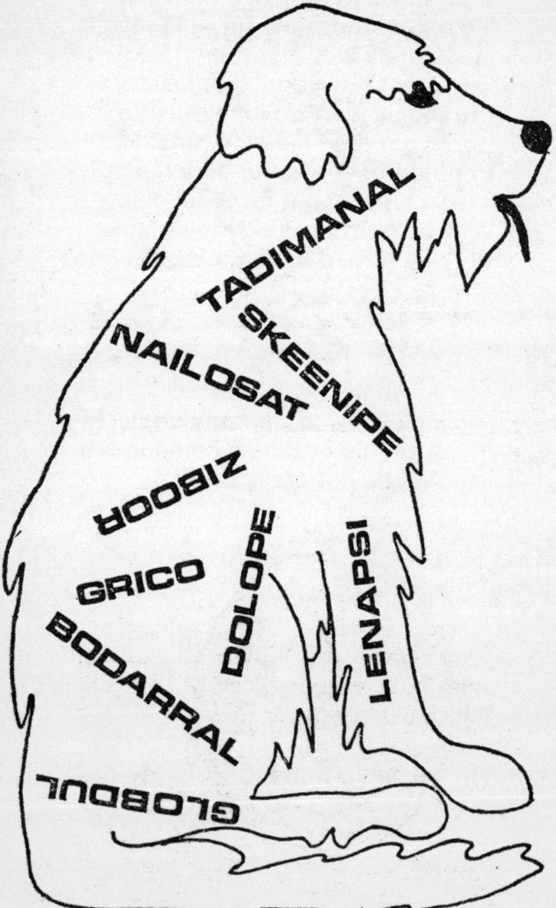

Don't Bank On It

'It's my firm belief, Butch, we are the victims of a practical joke.'

An Easy Combination

'I was working late, preparing an advertising campaign,' said Fellows. 'About ten fifteen I heard the outer office door click. Being unarmed, I hurriedly turned out the lights in my office and waited breathlessly, as there was a large sum of money in the safe. I knew my chances of attracting attention from the tenth floor were small, so reaching for the phone I hastily dialled headquarters and told them in a low voice to send help immediately. Then, creeping noiselessly to the open safe, I gently shut the door, twirled the combination, and crawled behind a big old-fashioned desk.

'In a few minutes the robber entered my office, flashed his light over the place, and went to the safe. He had it open in about two minutes, took the money, and left. That's all I know about it.'

'What time is it now, Mr. Fellows?' inquired Professor Stiggins.

'Why, I haven't a watch.'

'How, then, did you know it was about ten fifteen when you heard the door click?'

'I had gone for a sandwich and I left the restaurant next door at ten five. I had been back about five minutes,' replied Fellows.

'You say the burglar was masked,' continued the professor. 'How did you know that?'

'As he put down his light to open the safe, I could see the mask,' returned Fellows belligerently.

'Very interesting, Fellows,' smiled the professor, 'but you'll have to be a better liar than that to fool me.'

WHERE DID THE PROFESSOR DETECT THE LIE?

Thing No. 28

FIRST AID HINT

DO NOT MOVE THIS PATIENT

until you have tied his left shoe-lace. Overlook a little thing like that and he could end up in hospital.

A Head Start

Can you put the right hat on the right person?

stetson	priest
busby	policeman
fez	Mexican
turban	cowboy
bowler	guardsman
biretta	Indian
helmet	bishop
sombrero	Turk
mitre	businessman

Clowning About

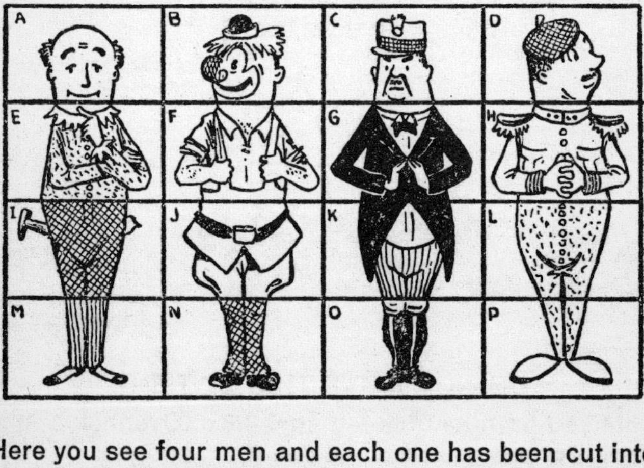

Here you see four men and each one has been cut into four pieces. These pieces have been mixed up, so that the men look very strange. Which pieces belong together?

Old Quin Queeribus

Old Quin Queeribus—
He loved his garden so,
He wouldn't have a rake around,
A shovel or a hoe.

For each potato's eyes he bought
Fine spectacles of gold,
And mufflers for the corn, to keep
Its ears from getting cold.

On every head of lettuce green—
What do you think of that?—
And every head of cabbage, too,
He tied a garden hat.

Old Quin Queeribus—
He loved his garden so,
He couldn't eat his growing things,
He only let them grow!

Nancy Byrd Turner

Food for Thought

Diner: 'Do you have a pig's trotters?'

Waiter: 'No sir. It's my corns that make me hobble this way.'

What did the doughnut say to the rolls?

If I had as much dough as you I wouldn't hang around this hole.

A cannibal mother and her little girl were watching the skies as a big airliner zoomed by. 'What's that?' asked the child. 'It's something like a lobster,' explained her mother. 'You can eat what's inside.'

Waiter: 'I have boiled tongue, fried livers, and frog's legs.'

Diner: 'I don't want to hear about your personal troubles. Just get me a cheese sandwich and a glass of milk.'

Mrs Smith: 'Well, Sammy, what are you going to do when you get as big as your father?'

Sammy: 'Go on a diet.'

One day, while driving in a thunderstorm, a man got a flat tyre outside a monastery. A monk came out and invited him inside to have dinner and spend the night. The motorist accepted. That night he had a wonderful dinner of fish and chips. He decided to compliment the chef. Entering the kitchen, he asked the cook, 'Are you the fish friar?' 'No,' replied the man, 'I'm the chip monk.'

Diner: 'This coffee tastes like mud.'

Waiter: 'So it should, sir. It was ground this morning.'

How's Your Arithmetic?

In this picture there are a number of numerals, and it's your job to find them all, add them together and get the correct answer. Difficult? Not at all! Try it!

Smiling Villain

Forth from his den to steal he stole,
His bag of chink he chunk,
And many a wiked smile he smole,
And many a wink he wunk.

Anon.

Tyred

A very old lady called Plotser,
A brand new 'Pneumatic' has got sir;
  She mounted that bicycle
  Cool as an icicle,
But when she got off she was hot, sir.

The Optimist

The optimist fell ten storeys
  And at each window bar
He shouted to the folks inside:
  'Doing all right so far!'

Anon.

Central Eating

Radi was a circus lion,
Radi was a woman hater,
Radi had a lady trainer
Radiator.

Anon.

Pick Pockets

'We're only sorry to have taken so much of your time.

Thing No. 29

COOKERY FOR GIRLS

Answers

Page 9

Plane Daft

1. Flag on right. 2. Handle of bag on right. 3. Woman's hat. 4. Smoke from cigarette. 5. Wheel of plane on right. 6. Hat of man on stairs. 7. One window more on plane. 8. Coat of man on right.

Page 13

Apeing About

Lapel, apex, trapeze, escape, aperture, shape, newspaper, gape, caper, cheaper.

Page 17

Which Way?

Up.

Page 22

How Many?

Thirty.

The Milky Way

First he must fill up the 12-pint measure. Then if he pours out from it enough to fill both the 4-pint and the 5-pint measure he'll be left with exactly 3 pints.

Page 26

Mixed Similes

As clean as a whistle; as busy as a bee; as innocent as a new-born babe; as black as the ace of spades; as sly as a fox; as deaf as a post; as stiff as a board; as strong as an ox; as pure as the driven snow; as daft as a brush; as blind as a bat; as bright as a daisy.

Page 31

Picture Puns

Shoe tree, gun dog, fountain pen, ear wig, tap dance, boxing match.

Picture Puns

Page 32

Hot house, a fork in the road, finger nails, box of dates, a football fan, dumb bell.

Page 39

Up For Grabs

1. Tie on peg is longer. 2. Feather on hat on right. 3. Cigar on floor is shorter. 4. Man on left has more buttons. 5. Man in centre has more hair. 6. Coat pocket of man on right is smaller. 7. One more coin on floor. 7. Vent in coat of man on left.

Page 46

UMP

Trumpet, umpire, Humpty Dumpty, plump, crumple, stump, Rumplestiltskin, jumper, hump, thump.

Page 48

Decoding

Bring your forces to battle zone. Captain Welsh hit by shell. Fatal. Help urgently needed.

Headquarters.

Dangerous foreign spy circulating in Buckingham Palace. Imposter must be apprehended before bomb explodes.

Page 52

Inspector Markham Investigates

There are wet footprints on the floor. The heel shows three holes and this man is the only one wearing heels with three holes.

Page 61

What Would You Like to Drink?

From left to right: apple juice, milk, water.

Page 63

A Military Parade

Numbers 2 and 4.

Page 65

In Other Words

Ash, oak, plane, pine, elm, willow.
Herrings, skate, haddock, carp, pike.

Page 66

Triangles

Thirty-five.

An Odd Problem

Just one! There are only two kinds in the locker and any one will match one of those he is already wearing.

Page 77

Word Squares

Flop, lop, pig, tin, tinsel, most, cup, zoo, rim, imp, knock, no, ass, pass, pet, law.
Easter, like, tot, prop, pelt, tip, air, skip, ten, tent, keep, trusts, rust.

Page 81

Pair the Words

Hairbrush, sugar tongs, book mark, shoe tree, block hammer, cobweb, paper weight, brief case, horseradish, pineapple, engagement ring, soap dish, blackboard, pin cushion, ink well.

Page 92

Dice Puzzle

Eight. You get the answer by adding together the sides of the dice that are not shown.

Page 96

Make a Pair

Bucket and spade, dustpan and brush, knife and fork, cup and saucer, scissors and paper, needle and cotton, pen and ink.

Page 100

Find the Truants

The boy lying across the heads of the two girls on the right of the teacher, with his head on the teacher's shoulder. The girl upside down in the tree.

Page 102

One is Right

The Eight of Clubs shown on the left on the bottom row is the correct one.

Page 105

Hidden Birds

Jackdaw, swan, nightingale, thrush, parrot, budgerigar, swallow, owl, goose, lark.

Page 109

Hung Up

1. Man on right wears bowler hat. 2. Smaller lamp. 3. Tie of man sitting on left. 4. One more picture in newspaper. 5. Woman's belt. 6. Man on left wears longer shoe. 7. Stop button lower. 8. Longer hook of coathanger.

Page 110

Two Coin Puzzles

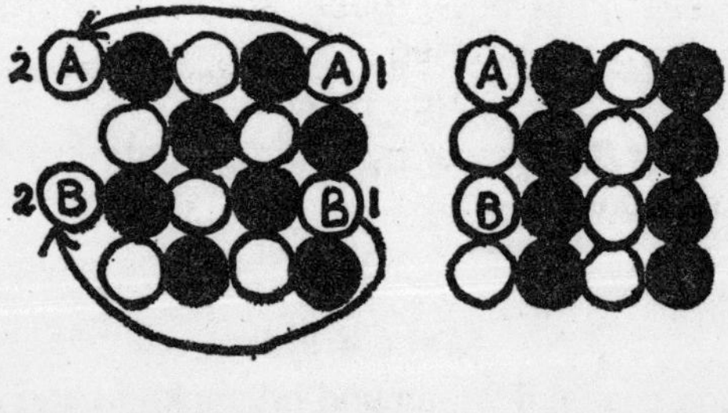

1. Put your fingers on coins A and B, as shown in Position One. Bring the coins around to Position Two.

Then push the A and B coins sideways to the right the distance of one coin, until you have a 4-by-4 pattern again. You will then have two rows of heads and two rows of tails, as shown in the second illustration.

2. Just add an odd number of coins, such as a 1, 3 or 5. An even number of coins on the table has now become odds. An odd number has become even.

Page 114

More Picture Puns

Alley cat, lamp shade, foot stool, a house fly, cloudburst, armchair.

Page 119

Inspector Markham Investigates

The injured artist was painting on Walsh's property. The brick wall illustrated in the painting is the same as the building on Walsh's property. The bricks of Ward's building are of a different size.

Page 120

Where Are You?

Tonbridge, Swansea, Newcastle, Manchester, Carlisle.

Page 122

Christmas Pudding

Raisins, suet, currants, peel, spice, almonds, flour, eggs, sugar, milk, nutmeg.

Page 124

A Triangular Puzzle

Page 129

OO?

Baboon, hullabaloo, zoom, voodoo, loose, sloop, foolhardy, typhoon, boomerang, marooned, cuckoo.

Page 135

Down Tools

There were 12 people.

Page 140

A Moving Puzzle

Lean, slip, hop, turn, sit.

Parts of the Body

Arm, liver, ear, leg, lung.

Page 145

The Cat and the Mat Puzzle

Mattress, smatter, tomato, dogmatic, intimate, diplomat. Catkin, scatter, locate, education, indicate, suffocated. (Other words will fit too.)

Page 148

Busy Bs

Boys, bikini, book, binoculars, bottle, basket, ball, buoy, boats, birds, bucket, bathers, balloon, beacon, bat.

Page 151

Climb the Ladder

Goad, glad, clad, clap, claw, flaw, flat, feat, fear, pear, peer, pier.

Page 154

Coins in a Row

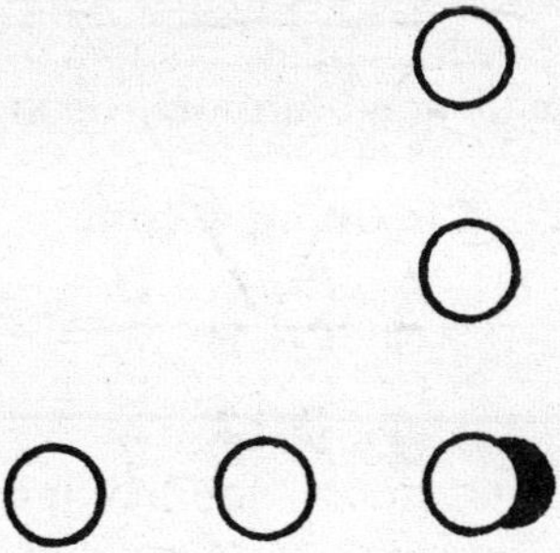

Page 155

A Circular Puzzle

Page 158

Crazy Mixed-up Dogs

Corgi, spaniel, poodle, dalmatian, pekinese, bulldog, labrador, borzoi, alsatian.

Page 160

An Easy Combination

It would have been impossible for Fellows to have hastily dialled a number in the dark. Try it!

Page 162

A Head Start

Stetson—cowboy, busby—guardsman, fez—Turk, turban—Indian, bowler—businessman, biretta—priest, helmet—policeman, sombrero—Mexican, mitre—bishop.

Clowning About

A	B	C	D
G	E	H	F
K	L	J	I
M	P	O	N

Page 165

How's Your Arithmetic?

The sum comes to 9483 if your arithmetic is correct.